THE LU[illegible] ONE

THE LUCKY ONE

SOME MEMORIES OF A LIFE

by

Mick Cooper

Moyhill Publishing

First Published in 2020
ISBN 978-1-913529-95-6.

A CIP catalogue record for this book is available
from the British Library.

Design and typesetting by *Moyhill* Publishing.

Moyhill Publising,
1965 Davenport House, 261 Bolton Rd, Bury, Gtr. Manchester BL8 2NZ, UK.

Dedication

For Don, Paul, Brian, Andy, Roy, Nobby, Fred and Don

Acknowledgements

Proofing and Pre-edit, Lynda Parry

Final Edit, Dave Allen

Cover photograph, Mick Cooper

Back photograph, Dave Allen

Inset photograph, Alan Griffin

Contents

Introduction

It has been suggested to me that I write my life story, but I replied, I'm a nobody, one of the many who almost made it. I can't imagine anyone wanting to read that?

As I write this, after some thought and finally deciding to do so, I am in my seventies. Looking back I remember many happy moments and days that I will detail below, also a few not so memorable that maybe I won't.

So here, somewhere between these covers, are a few memories of adventures and happenings from my earlier life that I have managed to drag out from the archives and pigeon holes of this old brain of mine. Hopefully you will find it interesting? And maybe amusing and they might even entertain you. I hope you won't think I have wasted your time or my lifetime.

One thing I am very sure of is that I am lucky to have been born where I was in Portsmouth, Hampshire and when I was. The NHS started soon after I arrived. I missed out on National Service and I am grateful for that. If I had to do my two years in one of the services it would have changed my life and I would have very different memories. Of course the trolley buses are gone and we now have one-man single deck buses. There are fewer cinemas, and pubs. Not so many music venues. However there are lots of new roads and motorways. There are many new buildings. The Cascades Shopping Centre where the Tricorn was and we do still have the Guildhall and the South Parade Pier, I'm glad to say.

We have a fantastic Ferry port and the City now hosts a fine University and together with the NHS is a major employer today. Some might question whether it's better or worse than all those years ago, but change will always happen regardless.

Music has been the oxygen of my life so here are a few musical memories. I have made money and had some good times playing music, so let me tell you a few of those musical memories.

I was born during the second world war and my earliest memory living at 18 Grenville Road in Southsea, a two up two down and outside toilet property, was listening to the Home Service and programmes like Housewives Choice, Uncle Mac on Children's Favourites, Victor Sylvester, Workers Playtime and Listen With Mother.

I just about remember meeting my father's parents, but my mother's parents died well before I was around.

I was told that my grandmother who was Alice Wilkins and became Alice Cooper on marriage played the piano, so maybe I got my musical genes from her?

My aunt May was my mother's sister and she lived in Lynn Road and we often paid her a visit. She had a piano in her front room which I would always seek out and attempt to make music. My parents hired a piano from Bennetts in New Road. I had piano lessons but sadly never kept it up.

I can remember as a 5 or 6-year-old, an occasion when my parents took me to see friends of theirs living in Powerscourt

Road. There were two young people there who were apparently keen on performing. They tried to get me involved in a performance in front of the adults, as families might have done decades before. I was so shy that I let everyone down and the whole performance in their living room failed miserably because of me.

Then in the late 1950's I was taken with friends to the Savoy Ballroom in Southsea. Here I had my first dip into the world of music and it had a tremendous influence. More of that later, but first I need to delve back a little further in time.

Schooldays

My early schools were Bramble Road, Francis Avenue and Albert Road. In 1952 aged about eight, my parents got me into a private school called Esplanade House School, previously known as Chivers. This school was started way back in 1830 by the O'Reilly brothers at St George's Square, Portsea. During the Second World War they were bombed out of the school which had relocated in Cottage Grove. It was probably then that they moved to St Bartholomew's Church in Outram Road Southsea as a temporary measure. Finally, in one of numerous locations, the school went out of business in 1966 at St Mary's Institute.

It did have some famous pupils including a City of Portsmouth Lord Mayor, Naval commander, Artificers, actors/writers and me.

My time at the school were in the hall along side St Bartholomew's church. It was a total shock and very much an awakening to what had been a dull life until then. I did not like it here or learn very much. I often got caned.

The hall had a very 'Dickensian' appearance and feel inside. The floors were bare floorboards and dusty. Trestle tables, four or five were set along each side. They were just wooden planks boarded together on an 'A' trestle at each end. The table tops were ingrained over many years with ink, biro markings and engraved scribbles along the veins in the surface. Hard wooden benches were placed along the sides each accommodating 4 or 5 bottoms with a chair at the wall end. At the top end of the hall was the masters desk and behind him a curtained stage. At the opposite end there were toilets and a store room. Eight or more boys on each table meant the room held about 60 or 70 pupils of assorted ages and educational levels and abilities. Charles Ashton Caine, known to all as Charlie, was the master here with Mr Morecambe, known to most as 'Moggy' in a next-door room with more pupils. On the wall near the door in, and the same door out, a large clock ticked away the hours. Sunbeams bled through the south facing windows picking out the particles of dust floating freely around the hall. Here I started to draw and my artistic side began to show. It was here that I failed my 11+. There were no sports, although I recall a single game of football was arranged on the Southsea common.

One day, I and a few others were playing football in the street nearby in the lunch time, and Charlie Caine walked by from home to the school and saw us. He said nothing but when we got to school we were caned and told football in the streets is against the law!

I did well at art and have a life long memory of struggling as I read my Euclid book and tried to understand what an isosceles triangle was! Another challenge was algebra! From those days to this, I don't think algebra has ever bothered me again. Around the end of 1954 we had moved house to 36 Blakemere Crescent Paulsgrove and in January 1955 I started at Portsdown Secondary Modern School. I was much happier here and learnt a great deal more as now I was much older, I could appreciate more. Here I played sport! There was football, rugby and athletics. I won a shot-put competition on the school sports day and had to go to Alexandra Park to compete but that day is forgettable, as I failed miserably.

I started playing the recorder and was drafted into the school orchestra by Mr Smith the music teacher. We did one public performance at the Baptist Church in Copnor Road.

I don't remember why but I started getting interested in table tennis and I started organising lunch time sessions, for a few friends I had made, on a large table in the science room. Eventually we managed to borrow a real table and I was being noticed by the headmaster Mr Lawrence. He was known by many as 'Puffer' as he had a habit of often blowing his cheeks out. 'Puffer' must have heard about what I was doing, and shortly after I was made a Prefect. The school had an ATC (Air Training Corps) Unit and I joined. I was an impressive sight in my uniform. We all went to Thorney Island one day with the promise of a flight. It would have been my first ever but the Gods were against us and the weather was so bad we ended up in a large shed watching people folding parachutes.

I began to get a feel for writing, and wrote a six or eight-page story in an exercise book. It was called 'The Forgotten Footballer' and I still have it. I showed it to Mr Gatt and then English master Jack Wells. Neither of them gave me much encouragement, so I had to guess their thoughts on it and my writing desires were shelved.

Probably around 1958 Mr Biscoe the science master made his class take a science test and to my total surprise I came top of the class and had my name in a report in the Evening News. Portsdown was by far the best of my schooldays, but of course being older now, I was able to realise and enjoy them more.

In the late 1950's music began to influence me greatly. I heard songs by the musical poet Chuck Berry and the musician Jerry Lee Lewis, and many others as something stirred inside me. I know now that, not having Grammar school intelligence, I was never born to be very academic. It was never in my genes to have 'loved' the high brow classics. The popular ones were fine with me. I tried listening to Shakespeare and the like, but it was always above me. The classy arts were beyond my understanding. Little did I know at the time that my real education was about to start in the University of Life.

Sometime around 1957 my parents and I had moved again to a flat in Patterdale House on Allaway Avenue in Paulsgrove. My father had taken me to see the football at Fratton Park in the early 1950's and I had thoughts that maybe that would be my future career. I laugh now knowing I was never good enough for more that a Sunday morning kick about although I did play a little football with a works team and cricket too. At school one day the metal work master, a Mr Harrison took the class for the sport/PE lesson. He was a rugby man and on that day I played my one and only game of rugby, and of course, very badly.

Many years later on a visit to Bradford I watched the Bradford Bulls rugby league team play and they won in the Odsal Stadium. There was a great atmosphere and it was a memorable day.

On leaving school at the end of 1958 I had a couple of shop jobs. The first in January 1959 was at Bowerman Brother in Osborne Road, Southsea. It was a very old traditional hardware store. Reading the story of Kipps by H G Wells where Kipps started in a Victorian haberdashery shop with a dominating manager reminds me of my short time there. Strangely, just a few years later I got the bug to read Wells' novels of science fiction and of a young man in a shop. It was a cold January and often old ladies would come in with empty paraffin cans and I, being the 'junior', would have to go out back into the shed and the end of their yard in some bitter weather and with chilled fingers fill the can and return it to the customer. All day I reeked of paraffin. I then had just a few months at another hardware shop called Asherfields at the top of Cosham High Street, but both were dead end jobs and I was restless. In April 1959 I started with British Rail at the Accounts Office in Goldsmith Ave. It seemed to be a job with some prospects of bettering myself and getting a pension. In Winter Road nearby was Tony Collett's music shop and I was a regular visitor there in my lunch hour. I bought a white plastic tenor saxophone and had lessons and attempted to get into music that way but again my interest waned and I gave that up, I realise now that was much too soon.

At sometime in 1959, once I had started working at the Goldsmith Avenue offices of British Rail, I again went with friends to the Savoy Ballroom on Southsea front. It was all new to me and it must have been about this time that music started seeping back into my head. Somehow, I knew that Don Golding who had been in the same class with me at Portsdown, was playing guitar in a group called Danny Raven and the Renegades. I remember going to sit and listen in when they practiced at the old Court Ballroom in Eastney Road. Of course this same room became the Birdcage Club less than ten years later. I went along to many of their bookings, and the music bug inside me grew stronger.

Whilst I was at the railways offices I met up with Roger Dicken, a Pompey lad who was working at a nearby department and we met in the old ramshackle canteen shed situated between two tracks in the goods yard. He and I both had song-writing hobbies. I remember us sitting there and looking at my copy of the New Musical Express. On it was an advert for a new single by a group from Liverpool and I said if these guys can make it then there's no reason I can't. They wrote songs and did quite well and of course that's Beatle history now. Sometime in 1962 Roger and I took a train to London to visit Pan Music in Denmark Street. We handed the guy there, one Gerald Benson, a handful of 3-inch magnetic tape reels with songs on. He didn't really like anything but asked who the group on the recording was. I mentioned the name The For-tunes, but little interest was shown, so we made our way home empty handed.

Roger was also very keen on horror movies and eventually moved to London where he worked on Dr Who with the BBC, Gerry Anderson's Thunderbirds and then created special effects on a number of well know successful films. For his monster model work on 'When Dinosaurs Ruled The Earth' he shared an Oscar nomination, but unfortunately that year the film was pipped to the post by the Disney production 'Bedknobs and Broomsticks.'

In late 1959 my father died and as a fifteen-year-old, I hadn't really had much time to get to know him, but on the 1st May 1960, (FA Cup Final day) my mother and I moved to a semi-detached house near the shops in Allaway Avenue in Paulsgrove. This was an important happening for me for which I shall be forever grateful to my mother.

My parents had years earlier tried to get me into a military music school at Deal in Kent, but nothing developed from that. Because I was in a dead end job I thought about joining the RAF and playing music there but I needed a qualification so signed on for evening classes at Paulsgrove School. Here I got to know about a few other local lads playing music and decided to seek them out.

Early Days

Early in 1960 I met Ron Hughes who played guitar and his brother Ken played drums and I told them I could manage them and get bookings. Ron and Ken and three others, made up the group. They started getting a set list of songs together with the intention on me their manager getting them gigs. Sadly I didn't have a clue how to manage anything, and strangely for me, the wallflower, I pushed my self into the young crowd totally clueless. For some unknown reason I decided to adopt the 'managerial' name of Clay S Kendrick. Laughable now but at the time I thought it sounded impressive and in fact it sounded more like a poor man's Larry Parnes! It didn't have much effect so was soon forgotten.

Eventually I did get the odd booking but that was not good enough. The first one that I do recall was one I didn't get. It was at the ATC hall in Goldsmith Avenue. It was situated was up stairs in a building next the Ricky's Club. Playing were Ron, Ken, Mick Poe on guitar, Barry West on bass and Lyn Appleton who sang. In later years that venue was used as a gym. The group played, 3 or 4 people turned up, including two I had brought from work, and that was the first experience of music on the road for me. Stairs became a big factor in my gigging life later.

The group had by now taken the name of Tony Wyell and the For-tunes, with Josie Franklyn. One evening I ventured into Paulsgrove School and spoke to the teacher who arranged gigs at the Youth Club there and got a booking for £10. It went very well. Mick and Barry and Lyn had left and Paul Spooner, who used the name Tony Wyell had joined and there was a change in girl singers. Veronica Lake had joined us and we decided she should use Josie Franklyn as her 'stage name' together with a new guitarist named Don David and bass player David Cawte. In early 1962 my mother had signed forms as guarantor for an amplifier on HP for Don and he took the forms away but before he could get the amp he was killed riding his motor bike one Monday morning close to the old Johnson & Johnson roundabout that is now a major cross roads. He was just 17 and on his way from his home in Gosport to work at GEC on the old airport site.

By now both Ron and Dave had both made their own pale blue guitars and they sounded pretty good. Soon after this Paul departed and we never heard much about him again until one day a photo of him and his wife and a new baby made the front page of The Sun newspaper. Apparently he was the first man in Britain to have a vasectomy reversed and stood holding the child to prove it!

Unfortunately Paul died in the late 1970's and oddly enough I photographed his wife's second marriage. It's quite possible that the child has their own children and grandchildren by now. Sometimes it's a very strange world.

The For-tunes

The precise spelling of the name The For-tunes or Four-tunes was never decided upon. I don't think we ever decided which way was best. Before they were called The Crickets, Buddy Holly's group were called the Three Tunes. We were all Holly fans, and as there were four of us it seemed the obvious choice!

We decided we should make some recordings and a mobile studio was found. Southern Sound Recordings had an office above the Avenue Artistes office at The Avenue in Southampton. The owner Peter Taylor recommended Hamble village hall for it's natural reverb and so it was booked. We recorded about 12 songs and instrumentals and it seemed as though we had our feet on the first rung of the stardom ladder. Here is the list.

1. Unknown (instrumental)
2. Little B (drum solo)
3. Why little girl (Pete sings)
4. I don't know (Pete sings)
5. Twisted bagpipes (instrumental)
6. My grandfather's clock (Pete sings)
7. Lergi part 3 (instrumental)
8. Ting a ling (Ron sings)
9. Island of love (Pete sings)
10. Teardrops fall like rain (Pete sings)
11. Patricia (instrumental)
12. Unchained melody (Pete sings)

From then on we got quite busy with work from the Avenue Artistes agency in Southampton.

The Savoy Ballroom on Southsea sea front was a very prestigious venue through much of the 20th century. It was built in 1929 on the site of an old lifeboat station. Many famous national and international names performed at the Savoy over many years. Two to mention would be the Stan Kenton Band and the Beatles. In the early 1960's pop groups were being allowed to play during the dance band's breaks.

I wanted to get the Fortunes a gig there. I was told that they would have to do a live audition one night and the fee for 'beat groups' was £10. All was agreed and the gig went well. Several months later I received a letter offering another booking, and was told that the group would have to join the Musicians Union first. I found out that the local Secretary was Reg Banistra who was the leader of a local dance band. I called at his mid-Victorian terrace home in Alhambra Road, just a few properties behind the Savoy building. I paid the money and we joined. We did the gig and I then went to the cash desk for payment and was handed £10. I told the cashier that I had calculated that Musicians Union members should be paid an hourly rate per person and that was £15 in total. The cashier telephoned the upstairs office and then said to me "Mr Turner said pay him!" The ballroom came to and end before 1970 when the whole block was taken over by Pleasurama and changed the name to Neros.

One night we played near Salisbury, in a village hall, and during the evening the van which a friend of Dave's had provided and drove for us was stolen by some local yobs and it was apparently found hours later in Salisbury Square! Meanwhile Ron and another stayed in the hall guarding the equipment and the rest of us were taken to Salisbury police station. A few hours later Ron's father drove up and around 3am took us all home. I think there were some court proceedings after that but cannot recall the outcome.

Our bass player Davie Cawte bought a bubble car and drove it round to Ron's house to proudly show it off to the rest of us. Just a week or so later we had a gig in Brighton and our van had broken down. We loaded all of us and gear into small 5cwt Ford van and Dave's Isetta bubble car. It was difficult fitting all of us and our gear in both vehicles. Dave, Ron and Ken drove off in his bubble car. The canvas roof had to be left open as they had to feed gear in through roof. There were two guitars sticking out of the roof with two amps on Ron and Ken's laps and part of the drum kit on back shelf. Dave could only just about drive but after loading and getting themselves in they couldn't get to the door handle in front of them to open it.

They set off for Brighton and when about half way there, Dave noticed a smell of burning and Ken started writhing around shouting in obvious discomfort. They thought he was joking, but then there was a lot of smoke and Ken started screaming loudly. Dave brought the bubble car to a halt. Somehow, Ken pushed the guitars out of the roof and managed to climb out. He always was a skinny lad. By now there was a lot of smoke and Ken was out, Ron and Dave were now able to open the door and jump out. By this time there were flames coming from the seat. They removed the hard seat cover and found the problem to be that the excess weight of the three of them on the seat had forced the steel seat springs down onto the exposed battery terminals and shorted out the battery. The seat springs had become red hot, setting fire to the horse hair seat pad, burning right through it. Poor Ken was jumping around in the road holding his backside still shouting "Oh my ass!" The red hot springs had burnt through his trousers and left painful burns on his backside. They put out the fire, covered the battery got everything back in and continued the journey and eventually got to Brighton on time.

Another regular trip was up the A3 to Bob Potter land! We were told that he had been a drummer in many dance bands since the Second World War and had recently retired. He also owned and ran a recording studio and an entertainment agency in Camberley. I think it was in Woking Town Hall where we supported a new singer who that day had a record reach No 1. His name was Tom Jones. All the girls flocked to his far end of the hall and we were totally ignored at our end. Unfortunately, Mr Jones never said hello to us.

I had a kind of longing to be in the group. I decided to get a keyboard from Bennetts in New Road and join in. Keyboards and organs were being used more and more in pop group recordings, and it seemed a good idea at the time. It was a small single manual single note organ called a 'Solente' ! I think I paid abut £40 for it. It was presumably made by a local company, but it was very limiting in its abilities. Having said that, most of my 60's music life I was just a chord player, and never really got into solos and improvisation. I was regretting not keeping my piano lessons going many years before.

The first gig I played was with that group at the Andover TA Centre in 1964. It was so forgettable as I was scared to death! Other gigs followed but very slowly I got into the 'group music scene.' Soon after this we were looking for a new male singer. Peter Richardson was drafted in and a new name for him was required. He said that at work he was always called 'Ritchie' so I re-christened him Ritchie Peters, thus reversing his real name. Shortly after I changed my instrument spending £200 for a Vox Continental organ, bought from Stan Bennett in Fratton Road, similar to the one used by Alan Price of the Animals on their "House of the Rising Sun" recording. We did some more recordings, this time at the Thorngate Hall and the Hillside Youth Club with the new organ and they sounded good. A year later I bought a 'Hammond L' and a Leslie Cabinet, again from Bennetts this time from Billy Bennett back in New Road. I seem to recall the organ was £500 and the Leslie an extra £300. As you may imagine, that amount of money in the 1960's was no small change! Percussion was added to the bass pedals at extra cost to make them sound more authentic but I never had any need to use them at the time.

Carrying this 2 hundred-weight piece of equipment was a pain in the backside and volunteers were always reluctant to jump at the chance to help. I lost track of the many times we got to a venue only to find we had to carry all of our equipment up and down a tricky flight of stairs.

Working as I did for British Rail, the secretary of the social club knew I had musical friends and asked us to play at a rail social club night but it was to be on an Isle of Wight ferry. Maybe you can imagine the problems getting on and off might cause but I don't recall any problems that we had. However my Hammond organ, when turned on, had a 'tone wheel' constantly rotating at one speed and this keeps it's tuning in concert pitch. The power supplied was not constant therefore the tone wheel wowed and fluttered and it sounded way out of tune. There was nothing I could do other than sit relaxed and just listen and watch. I think we were the first ever 'group' to play on the IOW boats. Sometime later they frequently ran Pop Beat Cruises on them. These ships were being used long before the present-day Catamaran Ferries.

The music we started playing was all the early 1960's songs, but that morphed into Tamla songs and then into blues numbers, strange but interesting, learning days! Now we were known as Richie Peters and the Original For-tunes. The 'Original' word was added as a group called the Fortunes had started making the charts. Then soon after it was decided a name change was needed and we became The Rampant. About this time my old school friend Don Golding joined the group on guitar.

We started doing a lot of gigs in the early 1960's courtesy mainly of Avenue Artistes. One of the regular trips was to the Pier in Lyme Regis. It is a pretty little town with a great beach and we always seemed to go over well here. One of our guys, who shall have to remain nameless got very friendly with a local girl. We were all invited back down there for her birthday party one Sunday afternoon at her home. As we left, the girl's mother handed us a large sponge and icing cake and begged us to take it with us and eat it when we get home.

We had problems getting to some gigs so Dave had bought a Bedford dormoville minibus which we used as a band wagon. It had seats in the back but we still managed to get all of our equipment, such as it was then, into the back and 5 or 6 of us in the front end.

On this day there were five guys in a bumpy rocking van with Ron holding a very fragile cake. He suddenly said to me "Open the door." We were travelling at about 30mph and slid open the door of our minibus. Ron noticed someone walking down the nearside pavement towards us. As we got near he heaved it out in an attempt to hit the passer by. Fortunately it missed and we drove on regardless in fits of laughter that must have lasted until we got home. I often wonder what that person said out loud at the time. Perhaps it's just as well I didn't hear.

The For-tunes had a booking down near Poole and we decide to take a camping gas stove and a supply of sausages and after the gig, stop somewhere on the road home and have a midnight feast. At the gig some of the guys got talking with a couple of very tasty ladies. We told them of our food plan and they said they knew the ideal place. Once the gear and the girls were loaded into the van we drove off for what seemed miles. At the time, we didn't realise but we had gone west and circled Poole bay and ended up on the end of a large slipway near Studland. Some of us decided to have a midnight dip. Soon males and females were down to their underwear and wading into the water and the cooking was started.

I was in the van and kept switching the headlights on. Little could be seen in the moonlight but in the headlights the girls looked good! One was particularly shapely. We hadn't noticed the large chains at the side and until they a started clanking. Someone realised that it was the ferry slipway that led across the mouth of the bay, to Sandbanks. Maybe it's better now known to us all now as Harry Redknapp Land. We had to quickly gather together all the clothing and camping gear and the pan of sizzling sausages and get off the slipway quickly or get run over by the passengers as they left the ferry boat. We laughed all the way home. I'm not sure if there is still a ferry across that stretch of water.

It was World Cup Final day 1966 and we had a booking that evening at Weymouth Pavilion. We all met at Ron's house on Portchester Heights and watched the game thinking we would leave at about 5pm and get the to gig on time. Of course it went to extra time but we had to leave. I had bought a small transistor radio and we tried to listen to the game in the van as we travelled. Probably because of the van's metal body and us moving the reception was very poor and we heard very little. Since then we have seen the game many times on TV.

Ron and his wife were living in a house in Wych Lane Gosport. The lease for the grocery shop two doors away was available and they bought it with his wife running the shop and Ron working at IBM in the daytimes. Ron and Paul Spooner had bumped into each other in Gosport and Paul explained he had been working as a painter decorator, so Ron promptly employed him to do some painting work at the shop. It was a small world even in those days.

These had all been fun and interesting days but I was becoming restless and had an opportunity to leave the Rampant and join others.

Soul Society

Just a few months later I teamed up with the Soul Society, and the most of the music was indeed soul, blue beat and ska. That included the songs of Wilson Pickett, Joe Tex, Sam & Dave, and songs including Midnight Hour, Sock it to 'em JB, and Al Capone. I did enjoy most of the music here and got on well with the guys.

The vocalist was Pompey's very own 'Mr Soul', Phil Freemen who is still singing these days. Phil's brother Roger was our driver in his Bedford van. It had the name 'Soul Society' proudly emblazoned on both sides. Some time later Stewart bought a green Ford Thames Trader van to replace the Bedford. Others in the band at the time were Stewart Ward on guitar, John Davis on sax, Ken Hill played drums for a time and then he changed to trumpet. So Graham Parker stepped in on drums, and Mark Hunter bass.

We practised at St Edmunds School in Portsmouth. However around a year later I was eased out and Rod Watts took my place. For a while I did nothing but was still working daytimes as a clerk for British Rail in their Goldsmith Avenue accounts offices. In total I did nine years in the offices of British Rail. Seven of them at the Goldsmith Avenue depot and the final two in the South Weston House very close to Southampton docks. This was originally a hotel where many of the Titanic passengers stayed before embarking on that fateful trip across the Atlantic in 1912. I had to travel to and from work by train each day, very boring but I did have a free pass. One of the accounts office staff organised a football team and we played about a dozen friendly games one year and I scored three goals in total. Office work was a drag and was not my thing at all, so in 1969 despite losing a pension, I left to become a professional musician.

Jamies Kin

It was back around early 1968 that I joined up with a group called Jamie's Kin. They included Nigel Baker, Jim Handley on drums and a bass player but his name is lost in my misty thoughts. There was also mod guy whose name is also forgotten and he was the singer. We rehearsed at a church hall in Westbourne on the Hants Sussex border near where Jim lived. A few bookings were organised one of which was at Kimbells and the support was the Bob Lambie Dance band and I knew him as he used to work in Bennett's Fratton Road shop. Music with Jamies Kin was not very memorable but one that stuck to this day was the rock version of 'You keep my hanging on.' My time with these guys didn't last very long, just a few months I think?

Heaven

Vic Brown was an old friend. I knew him from his visits to the Paulsgrove Grove Club several years earlier. In the music room there he ran the weekly music lovers group that met and loaned records from his own collection to play in the cubicles in a room there, similar to those in many record shops at the time. He was a bow-tied deejay at the Thorngate Hall and also ran jazz nights there. He was also the manager of the Universal Trash Band. I had heard of them. It was in 1968 I got word from him that their piano player was leaving and they needed a replacement. In hindsight I really think the fact that I still had my Hammond L was a big attraction for them. At that same time they were taken over for management by the MMF agency based in Gosport, Matthews, Martin and Ford was the full title. Vic was somehow eased out and Ricky Martin became the manager ably assisted by Ann Luckett. Ricky and a couple of the band got together and decided to change the band name. They had heard the song 'Everybody Wants To Go To Heaven but nobody wants to die' by The Karlins, a trio of singing triplets. Shortly after the name Heaven was decided on by the few.

The music played here was mainly self-written by bass player Brian Kemp and guitarist Andy Scarisbrick they were both very talented and they did write some very good songs. A splattering of west coast American music was also a part of the repertoire. Ray King was a clever multi-instrumentalist, able to play tenor and soprano sax, flute and penny whistle. Nobby Glover on drums was also very technical and excellent. That left Ray 'Ollie' Holloway on sax and Dave Gautrey on trumpet and flugal horn. He was also our sound man.

Ray King has reminded me of one particular night. We were travelling home very late after a gig and had dropped Andy off at his house on Hayling Island. Gerry Elmes was our 'roadie' and a former singer a few years earlier in a group called The Avengers. He and Ray decided they wanted to stop at the petrol station on the way off of the island as there was a machine for hot coffee and a machine for hot freshly cooked chips. Sadly those machine types are no longer around. There was also a cold milk machine in Drayton that we often stopped at for refreshment. On this night, a cup of coffee cost 6 old pence and a container of chips cost one shilling. Both Gerry and Ray have just enough coins for a helping of coffee and chips each. Gerry went to the coffee machine and put his six pence piece in.

Ray went to the chip machine and put his shilling in. The coffee machine delivered the coffee but without a cup so poor Gerry's coffee went straight down the drain. In the meantime Ray's chips arrived safely. Ray decided that he could eat the chips and then, after wiping out the container, he could use the same container for his coffee. He started on his chips and then Gerry put his shilling into the chip machine. Ray finished the chips and then got a coffee in a cleaned chip container. In the meantime the chip machine was making lots of frying noises. This went on for quite some time. Ray had now finished his coffee but Gerry still had not got his chips. Finally the container in the chip machine dropped down followed by a single, totally black burnt to a crisp chip! Poor Gerry that was not his lucky day!

If I am honest I sailed through these bands in the 1960's without much personal drive, ambition and direction. I just played what was needed. Again in hindsight the music in Heaven wasn't really my thing. Most of the guys were easy to get on with but as with any group of humans, the odd one seems to be a bit awkward and I don't think that was me. We did quite a lot of travelling to Nottingham and Scarborough and on one trip to Penzance and then two nights later in Holland. During the drive over night from Cornwall to the East Coast ferry port, we stopped at the transport café and Dave who did most of the driving wanted a rest. Just before we left a policeman stuck his head in our van and asked, "Where are you going?" He was very friendly and as he left us added "and keep smoking the pot!"

In Holland we played the Carre Theatre in Amsterdam and that was mine and our only gig abroad! Early in 1969 Ricky was unhappy with the way things were going and said he wanted to cease being the manager. We played at the Bishop Otter College in Chichester and the evening went so well that the whole audience applauded at the end and never seemed to stop. We would usually end with "The Worlds on Fire" originally by the American West coast group Strawberry Alarm Clock. Their version is about 10 minutes long. We had tweaked it and extended it to fifteen minutes or more. It always went down well. We were all so elated, and Ricky said "OH well perhaps I won't leave just yet!"

In July 1969 we played at a venue in East Sussex and it was not well attended. The organiser had brought in a small portable black and white television. That night we didn't do much playing but sat watched his TV and saw two men walking on the moon for the first time.

The songs the original HEAVEN (1) played???

Marjorine by Joe Cocker
The World's on Fire by Strawberry Alarm Clock.
If only the people would be the times or between Clark and Hilldale, by Love. (that is the correct title!)
Fresh Garbage, by Spirit
Killing Floor, by Electric flag
Smokey Blues Away, by A New Generation.
Evil Woman by Spooky Tooth, Canned heat.
Wear your Love Like Heaven, by Donovan
The Gardener, written by Brian Kemp.
Old Mad Walter, written by Brian Kemp
White Dove, written by Andy Scarisbrick

Recording in Heaven (1)

(There were three different line-ups for Heaven over the years)

Invisible City of Kartesh, written by Brian Kemp and David Gautrey
Bastard Child, written by Brian Kemp.
Old Mad Walter, written by Brian Kemp.
The Gardener, written by Brian Kemp.
Wear your Love Like Heaven written by Donovan
White Dove, written by Andy Scarisbrick.
You Will Be Free, written by Brian Kemp.
Our Plan For You, written by Andy Scarisbrick.
The Day That Judy Came To Stay, writer unknown.

The last song was given to us by Barry Kingston and was planned to be our first single release. None of us really liked it.

This recording was done in the basement studios of Southern Music in Denmark Street in London. Of course, that meant stairs down and then up again for my Hammond organ. In charge was Barry Kingston who ran Spark Records. Elmer Gantry's Velvet Opera was one of their successes and also New Generation. We made a number of trips up and down to London to record over the year or so that it took to lay down 9 tracks. Most of them were songs written by Brian and Andy. They were good songs. I was beginning to blossom just a little and managed to find a cute little organ riff to use in Brain's song 'The Gardener' In later years I recycled that same riff in one of my own songs and recordings.

Our trips to London for the recording sessions were mainly uneventful. However, on one occasion coming home at about 1am we got to just a little south of Guildford on a dual carriage-way, and a wheel of the old big SEB green van we were all in came off. Luckily for all of us the body work side panel kept the wheel nearly on its axle. This prevented it flying off into the air and fortunately none of us were injured. We ground to a halt on the grass verge and it was decided that Ricky, who always travelled with us, and was it Dave? would stay with the van for 'security reasons' and the rest of us would make our way home. This meant walking to the nearest railway station which was Godalming.

As we long-haired hippies shuffled our way down the country lanes in the moonlight to the station we were buzzed by a police car. It crept up on us from behind and as it passed they set off their very loud 'nah nah' siren and most of us jumped out of our skins. There just may have been a few rude finger gestures from us, but we were nice lads and we would never think of doing that.

At the station we realised that the next train south was the morning milk train at about 6.30.

We had 4 or 5 hours to kill sat on the platform. I finally got home at about 8 or maybe 9 am so had to phone into my British Rail works office and claim that I was unwell. I think I slept through the rest of that day. I am not sure how Ricky and Dave got on, but I do know they got home, the van problems were sorted and we were all ready for the next gig.

There was one annoying thing about playing music in Heaven, or should I say 'for Heaven', and that was when we first started. Because of the group name and the fact that I was sat at an organ, I was expected to and did, for a few months, wear a monk's habit. I hated it. Several times people would come up behind me and pull the hood of the garment off of my head. Years later I ceremoniously cremated it in my garden. We had been told that our recordings were hiked around a number of record companies but no one took much interest. Over the years we supported a few very well-known names including Status Quo, Jethro Tull, Deep Purple, T Rex, Idle Race and forgotten others. One thing people usually say about the 1960's is that If you remember them, you weren't there! Well I can assure you I was there and I do remember the 1960's very well. Yes there were drugs around, no names here! And I was offered, but never had any inclination or desire to find out or try any. Another strange thought is that although I have drunk lager at one time, I have always been a non-smoker and tee total. You may now be saying 'That sounds very boring.' Maybe it was but I saved a lot of money.

I do recall a letter being sent around to all the groups on MMF books signed by Ann Luckett to say that drug taking by any of their groups would not be tolerated. I still have a copy of it somewhere.

We changed our old SEB big green van for a much later vehicle with a separate cab and a large box arrangement on the back.

The back section of the box was partitioned halfway across and aircraft seats were installed in the front part with all equipment in the back end. Dave Gautrey was our main driver but we took turns to give him some rest times. I was driving back home from the Fareham area turning left uphill at Portchester into Station Road. Then as I turned right into Jubilee Road another vehicle appeared at the narrow junction from down that road. I was half asleep I'm sure and our vans off side and the car's offside front bumper scraped as I turned the corner. The elderly driver got out of his car and the expression on his face when he saw six hairy, hippie, young, rough and sleepy looking types suddenly surround him was incredible ! The repairs were all sorted out and I never heard another word about it! I can only assume that Dave and Ricky dealt with the insurance and repair and hopefully I was forgiven????

The Oasis in North End and the Vat in Hampshire Terrace were two Portsmouth regular playing venues for us as they were for many if not all of the local groups at the time. Of course both of them had stairs up or steps down and each time the Hammond had to be manhandled into the place. The Vat was a very small cellar and although full of atmosphere there were few members of an audience in front of us to play to. The Parlour, sometimes The Soul Parlour or Oasis and a few other names over the years was a more spacious venue. My claim to fame here was when we were supporting a name band whose name I have long forgotten, John Peel turned up and as he watched them he sat on my organ stool! Top that if you can! I don't recall who he was watching.

There were a number of venues where Heaven always went down well with the crowd. The Steering Wheel in Dorchester was one and also the Granary in Bristol and the Van Dyke club in Plymouth. At these places the audience would sit on cushions on the floor. After all we didn't play music you could easily dance to.

Within the year or so Ricky Farr took over and seemed to share management with Ricky Martin. We were booked on the 1969 Isle of Wight Festival the same weekend as Bob Dylan. On the Friday, Eclection were the first band on and we followed them. Bob Dylan wasn't performing until the Sunday but I never have been a great Dylan fan. I stood on the stage as they opened the gates and the crowd rushed up to the stage. I had an 8mm movie camera and filmed the scene. I handed the camera to Ricky asking him to film us on stage but he said he would be embarrassed and so it never got captured on film!

We did our 10 or so songs stayed most of the evening to watch others including the Bonzos and The Nice, and then were on our way back home on the ferry before midnight. It was an historic occasion for the Island and for us, but I don't think I realised that at the time. It was the only festival I ever played on and will always remember the privilege. After that Rikki Farr became more dominant and the group line-up was changed. In March 1970 I once again found myself 'bandless.' Ray King, Nobby Glover and Dave Gautrey were kept on and new blood was brought in. The New Heaven, (Heaven 2) sadly without me, went on the record the acclaimed album Brass Rock. With Ray, Dave and Nobby they brought in some others from the Southampton area. Apparently the singer later went to live in France and got group together and used the name Heaven, so that was Heaven 3.

So here ends my first 'almost.' So this is when a big door slammed shut and another was about to open on a very different world.

1970 Duos

During my Heaven days I had turned 'pro' and was signing onto the dole. I remember at that time we all took about £2 each a week from the group 'kitty' as a salary. As the New Year of freedom dawned, I had to find a day job. I started one day as a porter at QA Hospital and thought I had it made. On the first afternoon two of us were called to take a 'newly deceased' to the morgue. I went in the next day and gave my notice. Next, I had a driving and shop job with Comet in Palmerston Road. I soon got fed up with a daily struggle, finished there and became pro again.

I decided to take more control of my music and made decisions as to what I wanted to do. I found a drummer and we played some organ/drum duo gigs in local pubs. This time, the choice of all songs played was down to me. The bonus and the uncertainty was that I was going to be singing and now playing bass pedals. That was something I hadn't done at any time, but now the bass was down to me and it would be all evening.

I contacted a young guy called Mike Spring, a fair drummer and a little clueless about the music business. We bought a pair of speakers and he paid for them, several months later and out of the blue, I received a letter from his solicitor demanding I pay him back the money for them, which I did and then I changed drummers. Alan Fraser stepped in. A very likeable lad and we did work well together.

During 1971, I started going to a stable in Denmead with friends for horse riding, and enjoyed it from the start. The friends didn't keep it going. I began part time work at the stables. Early 1972 I managed to get on a three-month horse-riding course at Stocklands Equestrian Centre just north of Petersfield. Luckily for me, after a visit to the Job centre, the fee was paid for me. In order to qualify to take the final examination, I had to have educational merits. I took private lessons in English language and also music theory. I managed an 'O' level in English language and grade six in music theory and that was accepted, all at the age of 28.

At the end there was a test to obtain a qualification entitled 'Assistant Instructor' I gained 74 out of 100 but the pass mark was 75. I had no real intention of taking it any further as the wages for an 'AI' were low, but I did achieve an enjoyable and good standard of horsemanship. Maybe this was another 'almost' moment?

At Stocklands there was one horse, a pearl coloured large seasoned hunter that was actually called 'Pearl' and she was a beautiful and comfortable ride. Unfortunately I had been 'given' a horse to groom and look after daily called Trouper. Friends later called me Trouper Cooper ! I suppose it could have been worse! Sadly, Pearl is now long gone, and so is my back. From that test day to this I have never ridden another horse.

Geoff and Jim

Sometime late in 1971, I joined up with Geoff Davis and Jim Armstrong. The three of us did a few one-night gigs and Jim and I did a few without Geoff. It was in 1972 that we managed to get a residency at the Bishops Waltham Country Club.

This was an interesting, and in some ways, a very strange place. Backing cabaret artistes was needed for the many visiting turns and my skills or lack of them, was well put to the test. Len Canham who ran the entertainment agency Avenue Artistes was a regular visitor there.

It was here that we got to know the talented Lee Sutton. He was a drag artiste who wrote and sang his own comic very clever near the knuckle songs. Some of them were parodies. I remember he used the music to the song 'Grand Dad' and changed it to 'Drag Bag'! They were all very good. In previous years he was signed to the Joe Meek organisation and made recordings in his Holloway Road studio. The club was run by Norman and Eddie we never knew their last names, with Jean Harvey a heavyweight wearing a man's suit on the door. Lee recorded two excellent albums at the club.

After that in 1972 we found a residency at the Spring Inn in Sholing, Southampton. We did 3 or 4 nights most weeks and the place was always packed. Geoff had worked and performed for many years at holiday camps and other gigs. He sung, played guitar, did impressions and together with Jim we worked out some amusing routines incorporated in various songs we played. In one particular song called 'Running Bear.' Geoff would try to sing it normally but Jim and I would keep interrupting and infuriating his efforts. By the time we eventually parted, that routine had become a song of about 15 minutes! We also did a medley of songs from West Side Story, and Geoff seemed to enjoy singing 'I Feel Pretty', I never found out why.

We always liked to use different props in various routines and gags. When on stage, Geoff would thrust his fist down inside the front of his trousers. The audience could see him wriggling his fingers. A plastic chicken would be pulled out and held high and he would say "Have you all seen my cock?" of course it brought howls of laughter. On one night, he then threw the chicken with venom into the crowd. It fell on a table knocking glasses down and spreading liquid over on to a woman's lap. She hurriedly got up dripping alcohol and uttered words I'd never heard before and rushed out. We never saw her again. The Spring Inn lasted for 4 or 5 months and little did we know at the time but greater things were to come.

Jim was a very capable drummer but also could talk to an audience with ease. Geoff sang, played guitar and was also very happy to chat to an audience. He was also a very able fire-eater and comic drag artiste which he would happily perform in any venue. However a performance at Leigh Park Workingman's Club set off the fire alarms and the incident made the Portsmouth NEWS with a photo.

I think it was Jim's father Charlie who got us a residency in Clacton on Sea at the Highfields Holiday Park. Charlie was a true gent from the old school. He would help anyone without question, nothing was too much. This I was to find out some time later. For the summer season in Clacton it was decided to bring in a little glamour and Shelley Marden joined us, now we were a four piece. She was a shapely blond girl with a good singing voice and played a very modern keyboard.

It was my first summer away from home. I had never done a summer season before or been away from home and my mother for more that a few days. It was a strange feeling and Clacton was a charming little town with a beach and pier. That made it 'almost' like home.

The TV Comedians show had the season on the pier. We all went to see them and later socialised with them at a local bar. Geoff got to know Jim Bowen very well. They were almost like two peas in a pod.

During the season, I was often in Colchester in the daytime browsing around the record and music shops. For some unknown reason I decided to upgrade my Hammond L122 and bought a Hammond A. I had them split it for me at extra expense thinking it would be easier to transport, but alas, I think this one was heavier than the first! £800 was paid, if my memory is correct.

We played 5 or 6 nights a week and Sunday lunchtimes and lived there for the season in two chalets. They were very basic, with just two rooms and a small belling cooker. No bathroom but there was a public shower block close by. We did get home once or twice during our time there for a day or so. They were interesting days, lots of Londoners, lots of other entertainers and lots of temperaments, and also lots of pluses and minuses.

Also entertaining was a duo drag act Avis & O'Dell. Like many drag acts they did several different comic routines to recorded music, and were very funny. However, the 'entertainer's party' was nothing like those you may have seen on Hi De Hi.

Through the winter 1973/4 we did the occasional one-nighters. Also I did a spell with Frank Kelly and Steve Grant and we were called 'Frank Kelly and Friends.' Frank was a local boy and made a number of recordings for Fontana with a group of lads I knew called 'The Hunters.' In all honesty I really was not up to the type of music they were playing so left fairly quickly.

I was contacted again by Geoff Davis and with Jim Armstrong and we got our feet in the Pleasurama door and started at the Honky Tonk Bar on Southsea seafront opposite the South Parade Pier in the summer of 1974. Jim's dad Charlie had got us some gigs previously so again maybe this was his work? We were all very grateful. The years there turned out something like this;-

1974

Jim Armstrong, Geoff Davis and I started and worked there for just about 6 or 8 weeks in the summer of 1974. We were feeling our way a little but it went so well that we were asked back at the Honky Tonk for the next year.

1975

This time we were back there from Easter to mid September-ish.

We made good friends with many of the customers. Many of the ratings from the Dockyard ships British and American were also regular visitors, and some remain good friends to this day. Around about this time the bar was refurbished completely which made it more inviting.

1976

Back again from Easter to mid September-ish. Cabaret was brought in on four or so nights a week.

I think it was sometime this year that on one of my trips driving from home down to the Honky Tonk Bar I noticed my Transit oil light come on as I circled the Hilsea roundabout, and decided once I get to the sea front I would top up. However, half way down Northern Parade I heard some very nasty noises coming from the engine and managed to pull on to a side road. I began to panic. In those days I would never have thought of getting a taxi. Then it dawned on me that Jim lived quite near and maybe his dad Charlie could help? Luckily there was a phone box handy. I phoned and Charlie was soon there to give me a lift to the bar well in time for the start of the evening.

Some days after I hearing a mechanic utter the words "Cam shaft/Cam belt" and he tutted, sucked in air and shook his head, whist smiling and rubbing his hands together. A new engine cost me £300, which was a tidy sum in those days.

One day, Geoff brought in a small guillotine he had purchased at a magicians shop. He showed us how to 'fix' it and said he would get people out of the audience as stooges. I had to buy a supply of carrots to slot into the small holes along side the stooges head. It looked very safe, but somewhere in the back of my mind I could see it was an accident waiting to happen! Luckily it worked perfectly every time.

1977

Dave Knight with great vocals and bass and Chris Lowe, a clever left handed up side down vocals/guitarist came in and Geoff was made manager of the Honky Tonk. We four also tried to work out some amusing comedy routines. One was with Dave and Chris mimicking Millican and Nesbitt who were two miners who appeared on a talent show singing together. Dave and Chris wore white hard hats with NCB on the sides and bicycle lamps fitted and alight on them. All the lights in the bar were turned out and it gave a great effect and caused a few giggles.

I think our best on stage gag was when we all wore fancy dress and mimed to a medley of excerpts from four pop songs. I started it of with 'Monster Mash' dressed as Dracula. Then it was Dave who because of his beard and the fact he looked a little like Jesus, he walked out 'crossing' everyone and to the tune of 'Jesus Christ Super Star.' Next was Jim to the tune of 'If You're Going to San Francisco, wear some flowers in your hair.' Jim was dressed as a hippie. Then to the Leo Sayer song 'The Show Must Go On' Chris appeared dressed as a clown. It was quite a production.

One group who played at the bar about this time were 'Kiev' and their drummer was my cousin Tony Hawnt. Also another cousin who was ten years older than me loved to sing, David was fan of Al Jolson and was part of a group including former Heaven 2 sax man Derek Somerville. David would black up long before it was considered non-PC and sing Jolson songs. He was so dedicated that he had his name changed by deed poll to David Jolson. So there were other strands of music in my family apart from me.

1978

Geoff was always very versatile at the Honky Tonk, and enjoyed singing the good old rock'n'roll as well as a few ballads. One song in particular that he sang, performed many times and it always went down well was "Somewhere Over The Rainbow."

At the end of this year Geoff left the bar to do his solo bit on the country's stand up circuit.

Going on the circuit was a big challenge and he travelled the length and breath of the country in all weathers with many late nights. What a way to earn a living. Today he is retired and living in Spain where I know he has found that rainbow.

The four of us Jim, Dave, Chris and I continued ably assisted by Stan the man! Stokes.

We four of us played and sang well together. Dave had a great high voice and he arranged some clever medleys of Beach Boys and Four Seasons songs and we all harmonised well. Amongst others, one included was an instrumental medley of space film and TV Themes, which I particularly enjoyed playing. At the end of that year Jim, Chris and Dave together with Stan Stokes did some gigs elsewhere but I did not join in.

We had a routine where each of the four of us would have two Coke bottles filled with water which when blown were in an octave and we all stood up and played Amazing Grace into the microphone. It always was a good laugh and an achievement. One night Roy Castle who was doing a cabaret performance in Neros, just happened to be watching and he invited us up to Neros to perform that routine during his act. It was a very special moment. Sadly, we never got together with him, but I will be forever grateful for that thrill.

About this time also I had the desire to get yet another organ. I had found a music shop in Highfield Avenue in Waterlooville. Brian Lake was the owner and a very good organist. He sold me a Yamaha organ. The old heavy Hammond and Leslie went in part exchange for a much lighter easier to move model that was the same basic shape but lighter in weight. Hooray! It also had arpeggios and a drum machine along with bass pedals.

In the following years he sold me two more in fairly quick succession. With the second one I was able to use the two-piece lid as legs with its keyboard on top. It all packed down into a large heavy two man to carry box. "Oh dear!"

Next on the menu was a heavy Yamaha single manual keyboard, and this had everything at my fingertips making me sound like an orchestra. The bonus here was I had no longer needed to play bass pedals with my feet. Sadly, or so I thought at the time, it was stolen from the back of my Transit van when parked overnight close to my house. I had gigs on my books so again I made my way to see Brian Lake. Two keyboards later I bought a General Music keyboard and I still have it today! It was made by an Italian company and sounded good. The bonus here was that it could handle MIDI files. From that day on my song writing and recording blossomed, slightly.

1979

Geoff returned to the Honky Tonk Bar in Southsea for this season but this time we had new faces on stage with me. They were Fred Illingworth guitar and vocals and Nobby Glover on drums. Fred was from Bradford and sent down by the navy to Portsmouth to join HMS Albion. He was much older than he looked and we found out some time later that while on that ship he and some other ratings formed a group called 'The Four Jacks' and recorded for Decca. Hey Baby/Prayer of Love, was their single 45 vinyl. Other recordings were A Million Tears, It's a Lie, and Rainbow Road released much later on a CD compilation. He made no mention of it at all during his time with us.

I knew Nobby from 'my days in Heaven.' That phrase still brings a smile to my face. Back then he was an excellent and very clever technical drummer/musician and had recorded on the Heaven (2) Brass Rock CBS record album. So I was happy to suggest that he joined us. Strangely he was not quite on our level at the Honky Tonk. He was possibly too good for the clowning about we did each night. So after the first month Nobby left and was replaced by Mike King on drums.

Mike was a professional hairdresser by day and had played in many local groups over the years. He always seemed to be smiling and was a bit of a non-stop joker. He fitted in so well to our evenings with Geoff who gave him the nickname of 'Clump.' I think he must have dropped a glass of smoothing and Geoff called him that name meaning clumsy. But what ever it was the word 'Clump' seemed to stick for a few years.

We had by now a number different 'routines.' We still did the Running Bear song with Mike and me interrupting Geoff, but now it didn't seem quite as funny, so other gags were thought up. I made up a folding 'wall' of wood and hardboard which we used. Fred would slip the neck strap of a small blue man dummy over his head and stand behind the wall with his 'small blue dummy body' hanging over in front of the wall. Geoff wore a beard and they did a parody of the Smurfs hit song. The content was just a little blue, too!

Geoff and Fred would also do the Al Jolson song 'Sonny Boy' with Fred pretending to be a dummy sat on Geoff's knee and that always got laughs. The Stan Freberg song 'John and Marsha' was played with Geoff and Fred down behind the wall casually throwing items of underware over into the audience's view and the song went , 'Oh John, Oh Marsha' and getting more erotic as the song played to it's end. Geoff also did his stand-up gag routine most nights. There was a low ceiling in the bar so it was tricky when Geoff did his fire eating. It was my un-volunteered duty to get cans of Ronson lighter fuel for his fire eating sessions, always at my own expense. I would often visit newspaper shops and ask for a dozen cans. They always seemed to look at me suspiciously and wonder if I was just a heavy smoker or an arsonist. In his comic drag persona, he would walk on stage as a pregnant woman and mime to snippets of songs put together in a suggestive arrangement. Some of the lines would include Step Inside Love, Once I Had a Secret Love, then Something's Happening and There's Always Something There To Remind Me, as he(she) pointed to the belly bump. All a bit smutty and very non PC today and some gags were 'old style' too. Geoff was well into his routine of gag telling as we three, Mike, Fred and I, sat and stood back and listened. Suddenly Fred's guitar strap gave way and his guitar fell heavily to the floor. Unfortunately he had not turned the volume down. As it hit the floor a very loud discord of many notes resounded like booming thunder startling everyone one unexpectedly. Geoff went as white as a sheet with shock but quickly realised what it was, as Fred picked up the guitar apologising to Geoff and all. I suspect that most of the audience thought it was part of the act!

On one night a glass was thrown at him when he did some Irish jokes. Stewards rushed in and the thrower was removed and ejected from the building. The glass missed him, and me! Geoff's jokes and his routines always went down well and every night the bar was filled to the brim with people. Happy Days!

Once at some point, now lost in time to my memory, we were invited out onto on to one of the American aircraft carriers, the USS John F Kennedy. A liberty boat was arranged and all of our equipment de-rigged from the bar and loaded on to this little 'dinghy' size boat. Then the gear was manhandled up the side of a gigantic ocean-going ship. I still had my split Hammond and Leslie cabinet, and seem to remember 'not looking' as it ascended the side of the ship.

We set up in a hanger and played to an amused and bewildered looking audience stood around us. They also fed us and then we had to face the return journey across a small stretch of Solent water and got home safely.

The Honky Tonk was run by the Pleasurama organisation and other names to mention were Leo Leeson, a manager known for his nights in Joannas. Mike Allison was in charge overall and Clive Butler was also management. Clive had a very sporty car with the number plate CAB 1. In the last year at Christmas we attempted to do a pantomime on stage based on Cinderella, but renamed SINderella. With Mike King dressed as a fairy! Mike's wife Gina as a man, was that Baron Hard Up?, Geoff and Fred in drag as the ugly sisters, Fartingale and Ferkinshaw. Richard Podger as 'Superman' but known as The Incredible Sulk. I was in civvies, thank goodness, as the compere. One of the songs we used was 'If I Were Not Upon The Stage' with each of us then singing a rude parody verse. We actually got Clive on stage one night singing a verse of 'If I were not upon the stage!' I recall his line was:- If I were not up on the stage I wonder what I'd be, a butler I would be. You'd hear me all day long singing out this song, What can I do for you sir,... etc. No one made any suggestions.

One of the gigs that Geoff, Mike, Fred and I did in the winter of 1980 was to a corporate gathering in a grand old house in Stratford upon Avon.

I had no van at this time and Fred said he had a trailer. I fashioned a few pieces of polystyrene into shapes like our amplifiers and other equipment and jig saw puzzled them into a cardboard box the same reduced in scale version as his trailer. I was full of funny tricks trying to be pre organised and perhaps a little too clever? On inspection we decided it would not be man enough for the long journey there, and back. I contacted my old friend Nigel Baker who had a Transit so we swopped vehicles for a couple of days. I think he liked my Spitfire! The van needed constant top ups of oil there and back but we managed it. Our performance in Stratford was to what looked like an audience of corpses sitting up. We left very unimpressed!

This was our last year and we left sometime around September 1979. It was the year live music ended at the Honky Tonk bar as Dee Jays were brought in to entertain.

Stan Stokes was manager at first with Richard Podger chief barman? Richard took over Stan's job later. Finally at sometime Russell Spowatt came in as bar manager.

1980

If I'm honest, and I like to think I am, most of the time, my times at the Honky Tonk were the best part of my music years. Others came and went but I was there for the best part of six years. It's quite likely too that those others that were there would say much the same. Geoff was talented at all of his various entertaining skills and on form, possibly his best form, and was well liked by all that came into the bar.

I still have many friends from my music playing days, in particular the Honky Tonk, and I still get people remembering me, which is very nice. In those early days there, Richard Podger was the manager behind the bar and he eventually married one of the bar maids Carol McDonald. She later became a Bunny Girl at the Playboy Club in Southsea. They had an engagement party and Mike King very kindly, out of the goodness in his heart, provided them with a cake. As they both stood ready to cut the cake, Mike handed them a hammer and chisel. The look on their faces was one of confusion and disbelief. They soon found out that he had put two house bricks together and covered them with what looked like icing, but was probably Polyfilla?

I dare not guess what it really was. I think they attempted to chisel the cake and soon realised that it was a set up. Sadly no real cake was produced. The evening passed without any further 'trouble.'

Around about 1978 assorted cabaret acts were brought in on various night of the week. Frank Carson was one and also Squire Hayward. Another was a young comedian living then on Hayling, called Michael Barrymore. Also Roger Spencer, who was previously the drummer with a group called the Idle Race, and I knew him from my Heaven days. Geoff Lynn was also in that group but later of ELO fame. Roger was now doing his own one man show in cabaret. Shep Woolley was a Tuesday night regular. He was very well travelled and enjoyably talented performer, and still is. These days he is considered to be a Portsmouth legend. We also had a few specialty acts, one of which was a knife throwing act called the Cherokees. Considering it was on such a small stage area and with all our equipment spread over it, it's amazing how they managed to perform without the knife thrower injuring his lady assistant. Geoff Davis was used as a target a few times and survived the ordeal unscathed. Of course a certain area of his body was always the target. There were shouts from all after of 'Don't rub 'em, count 'em!'

Also, on one night a week we had male strippers and on another night female strippers. It was my task, which I hated of course, to insert the cassette tape they gave me into my machine and sit on the stage while they performed. On the cassette was the music they stripped to. I remember one occasion when a pretty young coloured female stripper said she had forgotten her tape, and I said I had a tape with music on that she could use. Unfortunately in my haste, I slipped the wrong cassette into the player by mistake and before I knew it she was on stage dancing to something very strange. It was a recording of the Sunday night BBC Chart programme with Alan Freeman and a run down of that weeks top 20. The first song was something quite danceable. I tried to relax and breathe again. They usually had three songs on a tape for their performance. The second song was Rolf Harris singing Jake the Peg! I cringed and tried to hide myself. Next there came a traffic report about a large truck stuck across two lanes of the M1. She danced and stripped on. The final disgrace was Danny Kay singing 'The Ugly Duckling.'

I was mortified and my face had turned to a very deep shade of tomato red. She strolled off at the end without saying a word to me. I was expecting a very angry lady with a loud voice and swear words, but there was nothing. I rushed to the dressing to apologise. It wasn't to get up close to her with no clothes on I promise. I apologised again and again. She was very sweet and said she didn't realise and it didn't matter anyway. Maybe she was deaf? We all fell about laughing for days at my expense.

Another regular customer we had was an elderly gent whose name we never got to find out. He was always very friendly and chatty with us and always sat in the front row when the female strippers were booked.

The girls would use all manner of things in their acts. Usually they used baby oil and sometimes talcum powder. One night a girl who had sprinkled her chest with talc got off the stage and went up to this guy and pushed his face into her chest shaking her shoulders and breasts and then she got back on stage and continued dancing. The guy's face was covered in talc making him look like a gobsmacked white eyed panda bear.

It's quite possible that his days at the Honky Tonk were the best and happiest days in Geoff's working music and entertaining career, they certainly were in mine.

It was whilst I was at the Honky Tonk, a found my days were free. I had always been curious about my family history so started researching at local establishments as well as travelling to far off distant record offices to do this. On my own name I managed to get back to the late 1600's and with other family names back to the early 1700's. It is one of those hobbies that never seems to end. There's always more to learn about your ancestors the deeper you look.

All this led me into the 1980 when I decided to find out a little more about the history of Portsmouth Football Club. I had seen the 50-year 1948 small booklet which gave a little historical information but I needed more.

I started making trips two or three times a week to the Central Library and spending all day there. In those days one could actually look at the original newspaper from their store room. Today it's all on micro film at the library or partly on line. I went through newspapers from around 1890 page after page up until 1984, jotting down all the stats I could find, games played, teams, scorers etc. I must have spent the best part of two years several times a week in that library making notes and gathering history.

In the early 1980's a local publisher called Milestone got to know of my research and with another friend Doug Robinson connected us to the Portsmouth NEWS Sports Reporter Mike Neasom. I handed much of my information to him and he drafted out a complete history in text which became the first half of a book with my stats on blue pages in the second half. It was published in 1984. We had a big publication day celebration at Fratton Park. I walked onto the pitch and released a number of balloons that didn't move. I met John Deacon and a number of the players when we did book signings in shops in the following months. I believe Milestone printed about 16,000 and I today see them show up regularly on Ebay. It was a very memorable chapter of my life.

During the 1990's, the Association of Football Statisticians published an update of the book. The stats were in grid form detailing games played and team line ups etc, onward from 1985.

I had very little to do with it but they credited me and my name appears on the cover. I think only about 100 were printed for their members, so I never expected any fee.

In 2000 I had another football book published. This was an A to Z of Portsmouth FC Players and staff with photos, again all from my earlier research and I think only 4 or 5 hundred were printed. It bombed and I remember seeing it on sale in a shop in the Cascades Centre for £4. The book had been 'remaindered' which I think mean all the stock sold off at cost price.

That was finally and definitely the last of my football books.

I did only solo gigs in the 1990's and one every kind agent offered me three gigs at local military venues entertaining the civilian staff that worked at each place. The first was at Tadworth. I got paid so they must have liked me. For the next one, I played at Fratton Park ! Music not football, oh well, you can't win them all, ask Pompey! And the third was to be at a very grand and swish building in a road that backed onto and parallel with Oxford Street in London. I always like to plan ahead. As I always travelled alone, I said that I would do it if the venue could guarantee me a place to park my Transit whilst I was inside entertaining. Of course in central London that is impossible so I didn't get the job! It's tough at the top!

South Parade Pier

When the Honky Tonk days ended Geoff did a few solo gigs and drummer Mike King and I looked for work as a duo through the winter of 1979/80. One job was from the Ann Luckett Management agency. Ann was formerly of MMF and Stage One, and now running her own agency.

We were booked for a one-nighter on an Isle of Wight ferry docked in Portsmouth Harbour Station. We were told the boat would not move. Geoff who was free that night asked if he could just sit in and play rhythm guitar and we were happy to let him. When we got to the station we found a high sided luggage frame on trolley wheels and managed to get all of our equipment on it. Pushed it down to the boat and luckily the gangway was wide enough to wheel the trolley up and onto the boat easily. The evening went well and I briefly felt some movement in the boat but ignored it.

As we packed and left we saw that the wide gangway had been replaced with another that had hand rails only about 2 feet apart and almost impossible to manage with our bulky and heavy gear. The only way we could get my Yamaha organ, the size of a small upright piano off the boat was to slide it horizontally on its back along the rails with me at one end and Mike at the other. Just one slip by either of us, and more than likely me, would have sent my precious instrument to a watery grave! I wonder if Davy Jones in his locker is musical? However, we did manage to get everything off with some sweat and effort and eventually we all got home to our beds.

It was also in the early 1980's that I thought about a second occupation. I had dabbled with cameras while at Portsdown School, and then in the early 1960's I was a regular at the Grove Club in Paulsgrove. They had a camera club there run by a Mr. Cross who was the owner of the photo/chemist shop in the Guildhall Square. I got well into and enjoyed some success in the developing side of the hobby.

I decided to get back into photography, so I joined the Portsmouth Camera Club. Those days were very enjoyable and I got onto committees and helped with organising all manner of events including the annual Photographic Exhibition.

I fashioned a dark room in the front room of my house and bought all the necessary equipment for processing black and white photographs. It was a messy and exacting hobby but chemicals would 'go off' after such a short time and new ones had to be bought. What with all the equipment and cameras, it wasn't a cheap hobby. I soon got fed up of struggling in the dark room when I started photographing weddings professionally. I always sent my films off to a professional processing company, which was much safer. I met a lady, Tracy Rose, who organised weddings and did catering. She kindly gave me lots of work for a number of years. I got on well with people and the confidence gained in my music days helped enormously. Most of the weddings were enjoyable with the odd one or two being a little awkward. I photographed some notable people, including a 'Sir' and his lady. Also with another couple I photographed, several years after, the groom stabbed his wife to death, and he later died in prison in middle age.

I continued photographing weddings for 25 years from around 1982 to 2007. That was an extra income for me.

Eventually I was voted Chairman of the Camera Club for one year but after that I seemed to lose interest and I wasn't voted onto the committee. I had been a member for about 18 years. Maybe I had upset somebody? Another door was closing and I was looking around for another interest. This time it wasn't a door that opened but it was the curtains of the Kings Theatre, Southsea, opening wide and in 2000, I found myself on stage!

In the summer of 1980 Mike and I, now known as the Gee Dees, which was Geoff's initials, managed to get a season on the South Parade Pier courtesy of the agent Chris Lynn. Here we did five nights and Sunday lunchtime in the Albert Tavern. This gave us some free days for any other gigs but getting gear on and off the pier was always a drama! Here we met many of the locals and got many of them up to sing. There were about six or so people who always turned up and we got to know most of the regular customers very well.

I think it was sometime in 1981 that we managed to get an afternoon gig at the Portsmouth Guildhall on the big stage. I had been there many times to see shows, but this was my first time playing there. Shellee Lee was a popular local lady singer with a great voice who we knew well. She had sung with us on many previous nights and we knew her music. We invited her along and she was excellent. The session was very enjoyable and many of the crowd were older people and so our old time sing-a-longs went over well. Once we had packed up and Mike and Shellee had gone, I went back in and just stood on the bare stage looking out at an empty auditorium just soaking in the atmosphere. I was remembering the history that this building and its predecessor contained. There were so many international and national very talented entertainers and artistes who had performed there on this very stage on that very spot where I was standing. I felt a very warm feeling rushing around my body and so humbled. A City I was born in, this was my Guildhall and my Portsmouth. It was a deeply special moment on such a special day.

The Gee Dees played many of the local working men's clubs British Legions and various political clubs and we managed a fair income and mileage and many of the bookings through the John Bedford agency. We were also playing many after-noon pensioners gatherings. One such day at the Guildhall in Southampton after a gig an elderly lady came up and spoke to me. She smiled and said I know why you are called the Gee Dees. I waited expectantly totally oblivious of what she was going to say. Then she said "It stands for Geriatrics Delight!"

We were lucky and managed to stay on the Pier for the summer of 1981 and 1982, sometimes lugging our gear into the Gaiety Lounge, the home of legendary DJ Steve Kingsley, to back talent and beauty contests and some cabaret. The Gee Dees last gig was on New Years Eve 1982 at Hove Town Hall, so in 1983 again I was looking for a new drummer.

Drummers

In 1984 I went out singing and playing my Yamaha organ still playing bass pedals. I decided I needed a new name for my future public appearances. Often when I got to a venue, some joker would shout 'Here's the man with the big organ' or something very similar. At first everyone laughed. On the tenth and twentieth time one grinned through ones teeth and tried to ignore it. On the one hundredth time I felt like killing someone, but that's not allowed!

I decided to be positive and use the name Morgan which was my first name initial 'M' and the word organ. Often people would then say 'Here's Mickey Morgan with his big organ.' OK, I could laugh at this and if that phrase was remembered then my name would be in the Social Secretary's mind, and hopefully a re-booking might happen. I am sure it worked out that way some times.

Several drummers helped me out over the years, among them Ron Lang, Dave Petley Harry Gray, Ernie McBurnie to name just a few. There were also two local guys who are legends, Roy Huggett who ran the Drum Centre in Elm Grove, but sadly he lost his life driving home after a gig. The other 'Legend' was and still is the very excellent John Hammond. He is an amazing drum teacher and has played in all manner of music groups over many years from duos with me to the pit band at the Kings Theatre. A regular gig for him in recent years is with the Dave Pearson Big Jazz Band at the Blue Lagoon, Hilsea Lido. At this time I also did a few solo gigs. I didn't need a drummer as the organ took care of that playing both drums and bass. It was also another way of testing the waters. Firstly to see if there was demand and that I could find more solo work, but also testing me. Working alone is very definitely not the same as working in a group. Firstly, one has to move all the equipment ones self! "Ouch!"

But I managed it OK for a while and gradually got into a routine of doing solo gigs. Who would have thought that a young kid so embarrassed all those years ago, could now go out on his own and get people dancing and entertain them.

After a few years as a duo, I bought a single manual keyboard. The old Yamaha was large and difficult to move around but the keyboard was a great deal easier to deal with. Of course, I still needed amplifiers and all manner of other odds and ends including a PA system and assorted cases of wires and of course a van to transport it all. Sadly, many clubs were closing down and with those that remained I noticed the membership seemed to be getting much younger as the years passed by. Much of the music I was playing was becoming out of date and I was finding it very difficult to keep up to a reasonable standard. I could see that my musical days were running out. Photography was also changing from the old film cameras to digital cameras. If I had kept going I would have had to spend big on new equipment. My gear was also beginning to give problems. So that was another sign of more passing years.

One of my regular music trips was to a couple of former theatre bingo halls in Brighton.

Sometime in the late 1980's there was an important royal occasion and a public holiday. As the streets were very empty I managed to park my van outside the bingo hall. The manager there was Mike Allison who had been the boss at Pleasurama. It went well and they booked me back again some months later. This time parking was impossible. I drove for some time until I found a space, and then realised I had lost all sense of direction. I wandered down so many streets clueless. Eventually I went in to a shop and bought a street map and finally got back to the hall an hour after I should have started playing. I was almost in tears but managed to gather myself together and play a couple of sessions and they reduced my fee.

It must have been around the year 2000 when John Bedford gave me a solo New Years Eve gig at the Worthing Pavilion. I had only a few years earlier seen the Crickets there on stage, so was just a little more elated than usual to be on that same stage. I had got to know all of the Crickets when they toured here previously. I got all my gear in a set up then went to the bar. All I ever drunk at gigs was tap water.

I asked for a glass and was told it was one pound! Usually I got it for free. I refused it and turned away in disgust. Fortunately I had a bottle of lemonade in my van but of course that always makes you burp and that's not a good thing when you are singing. It was a local 'Lyons' function and I had to support a traditional 40's/50's eight or ten piece dance band. I played the first 45 and some people did attempt to dance, but there was little action otherwise.

The band did their spot and not a soul ventured onto the dance floor. I then went back on knowing this would be a struggle so decided to ramp it up a bit, as far as a solo keyboard man could do. To my amazement the dance floor was busy and then busier. The band came back on and again no one danced. One of the Lyons committee came up to me and asked me to play extra time and we negotiated an extra fee. I was very happy with that. I played again and people danced until around 1am. The evening was a success. As I drove home through the streets of Worthing a speed camera flashed me and quickly deflated me. I never did get a summons!

The next morning I got up late as the phone was ringing and it was John Bedford, and he had heard from the 'Lyons' how well it had gone and praised me.

Vans

Over the years I have had to buy a number of vans. The first van and vehicle I ever bought was a Morris J Van, bought from a dealer in Fareham around 1963 for just £60. It had an engine under a bonnet inside the cab alongside the driver! A floor gear change and a gear stick about a yard long. It sounded like a tractor when driven which I did sometimes try to drive a few times with L plates before I had a license. It was very battle scarred and noisy. I tried to paint it with lead paint, and it looked awful. Later it was painted blue, but was always difficult to start, so probably within a year it was disposed of. After that for many gigs we hired a Ford Thames Mini bus from Denis Sims who ran Southsea Entertainments.

I bought a van from Ron Hughes. It was a Ford Thames Trader, which did great service, but when we got a residency I swopped it for a Triumph Spitfire sports car. That wasn't really a sports car but just a Triumph Herald with twin carbs! But it looked good and so did I in it! (Or so I thought!) At this time I was resident at the Honky Tonk and had no need for a van.

Later I had a few different Ford Transits, as I was by then just going out duo and solo, and finally a Vauxhall combo smaller van as I didn't need space for drums etc. These were usually bought from Southern Self Drive and were white so I always had them re-sprayed Pompey Blue.

Godchildren

In the 1980's I met Keith and Carol a couple whose marriage I photographed and we became life long friends. They gave me the enormous honour of making me Godfather to their three children, Antony, Rebecca and Mary. They are now all adults with their own families. I never had a family of my own so this gesture was an amazing kindness for which I will be forever thankful.

World tour

In 1991, I decided it was time to travel. Here I was in my forties and had never flown before. So I booked a non-musical world tour through Thomas Cook. I left Heathrow on my first ever flight. I asked if I could go up to the cockpit and was allowed. I asked the pilot where were we? He pointed to his screen saying 'We're over the Black Sea.' We chatted for a minute or two then I returned to my seat. We landed briefly at Singapore and then Sydney before stopping at Melbourne where I stayed for about a month with cousins who lived near by in Dandenong. The city of Melbourne is really very nice and I managed to get around on my own quite easily. Of course, I found the close where they made the Neighbours TV programme, and also managed to meet an actor called Paul Cronin, who played Dave Sullivan in the 'Sullivans' TV series. I loved those shows and was so pleased to meet him.

After a month in Aus, I travelled onward from Melbourne to Sydney and then across the Pacific Ocean to Los Angeles. Somehow I had missed my connection at LA. I managed to rearrange another connecting flight but it wasn't leaving for about another 12 hours.Through the night I sat and dozed a little. The airport became empty and very quiet. After a time, I needed the toilet, or to be more accurate, the cubicle. It was during Saddam Hussein's Middle East gulf war and security across the USA was very tight. I was unsure of what would happen if I locked myself in a small room with my cases outside unattended. I had visions of squads of heavily armed uniformed soldiers, surrounding the trolley and blowing my cases out of existance. I decided to wait. As soon as I boarded the next aeroplane the world was a happy place once more.

This time we were on a detour heading for Chicago. After a quick change of flight I finally landed in Nashville. My week there started with a tour bus ride around the area. As we started the tour we passed by a cemetery with a limitless number of military grave headstones, an unbelievably shattering sight. Then I actually sang on the stage of the Ryman Auditorium, where so many great country singers had sung together, but I was with the rest of the bus tour party, and we all sang 'You are my sunshine' together. The tour guide said "Now you can tell everyone back home that you've song on the original Old Opry stage!" We also stopped, and I stepped on to the 'star circle' of the NEW Grand Ole Opry stage. It is a much more modern building on the outskirts of the city. That was an amazing feeling. I saw the Friday and Saturday night shows there and even managed a trip down to Memphis and the Sun Records studio and of course, Gracelands.

Over the years with my interest in the Crickets I had met them on their tours here and in particular got to know Sonny Curtis well. In 1990 I organised a concert at the Ferneham Hall in Fareham with a British country singer named Kelvin Henderson. He and his band and Sonny Curtis performed that night. It didn't make any profit on the door but I was happy to have the memory of a great night. Sonny had said that if ever I was in Nashville to phone him, which I did. He lives just about 20 miles away but drove in and took me on a tour pointing out all the celeb homes and places of music interest. The journey home via New York was easier. Since then I have been to New York a few times and seen a few Broadway shows. I also spent a week with friends in Los Angeles.

All was fine there. However on one day we took a boat trip to an island called Catalina, about 25km from the USA. It was idyllic location with a quaint old village called Avalon. It had a great atmosphere and picturesque harbour. Nearby is the Casino Ballroom where in the 1930's and 1940's all of the big bands, Miller, Kenton, Dorsey and so on played there. Sadly there was one major problem there and that was what they called yellow jackets. The island is plagued with them. We sat in an open fronted beach café to eat and were constantly dive bombed by the wretched creatures. I never could stand what we call wasps.

Agents

Through the years, the various music outfits I have been in have worked for most of the local agents, and one perhaps a little more than the rest and that was John Bedford. He is now retired but told me once when he lived in London before moving to the South, he was signed to sing for HMV. I presume he meant the record company and not the shop, I never did find out the answer, or whether or not he was having me on. Other agents who gave me work were KM Entertainments run by Ricky Martin and Pete Cross, with inspiration from Steve Kingsley, Les Hart, and also Ann Luckett Management. Pete Cross later ran his own agency from home and booked me for my last ever gig at the Red Lion in Fareham.

In the 1980's Len Canham said to me that if I can join Equity the actors union, he could get me film and TV extra work on local productions. This I did and can be seen very briefly on a number of those old shows. I eventually became Treasurer of the Equity Wessex branch.

Of course if you join Equity you have to register your professional name with them. None of the names I'd ever used were acceptable, so another had to be found. In the end they and I settled on Max Morgan.

Here are just some of my ? moments, between 1983 and 1999.

June 83	Mansfield Pk. (B.B.C.)
Aug 85	Monocled Mutineer.(B.B.C.)
Aug 8	Howards Way. (B.B.C.)
Feb 86	Bobby Davro Show. (T.V.S)
Aug 86	Cats Eyes (T.V.S.)
Jul 87	Casualty (B.B.C.)
June 88	The Gor Saga (B.B.C.)
Dec 88	The Bill (Thames)
Feb 89	Sleeping life (Ruth Rendell Mystery) (T.V.S.)
Nov 90	Bergerac (B.B.C.)
May 92	Miss Marple (B.B.C.)
July 92	House of Elliott (B.B.C.)

Along sidesuch celebs as Jill Gascoine, Leslie Ash, George Baker, John Nettles, Joan Hickson, Richard Wilson, Paul McGann, Cherie Lunghi, Charles Dance, Philip Madoc.

Retirement

At the end of 2008 I played my last gig ever on Christmas day. And several months earlier I had photographed my last wedding.

I was happy to put it all behind me. It meant that many of the pressures of making money had gone, and that was a relief.

My back had been giving me some grief and I put it down to a bad posture leaning over playing all of the keyboards I had owned. Maybe also a little because of my horse riding days and then there was tap dancing, but that's another story. Now that I again had time on my hands, I returned to my researching mode.

On one day somewhere, someone mentioned to me that you can get lots of information on the history of Portsmouth, in books about the pubs, the cinemas and theatres, the Dockyard and yes the football club. However there was nothing about what I had spent the best part of my life doing, and that was the history of popular music in the City.

I again got into the habit of spending a few days at the Central Library to see just what was available. On one of those days, I was sat there merrily flicking through pages on a microfilm machine when I recognised a face that walked by me. I could see that he did also recognise me. Dave Allen and I got chatting and it seemed that he was on a similar task. He had been in several 1960's groups, Rosemary and Harlem Speakeasy and many more since then. We had met briefly in those days but not since then.

We agreed to keep in touch.

I went home with all the information I had gathered and started my Portsmouth Music Scene web page. My good friend Mike Gregory showed me how to set up and run a simple web page, and I have added all manner of items made available by many good friends. Items that came to hand included photographs, tickets, news paper cuttings, recordings and much more. I also had my own collection gathered over the years.

I am very grateful to the many people who have made their own memorabilia available to me. Some people have asked why do you bother with that old stuff, why not just forget it?

I believe it would be a travesty and a great loss if the history of popular music in Portsmouth was not recorded and kept. I have enjoyed looking back over the years, and of course I'm not too keen to look too far forward. Dave was also very keen on researching the 1960's music of Portsmouth.

Soon after I started, they had to close the Central Library building as taps were left on and the building was flooded. All of their film readers and other information was moved to a room in the museum. I say 'room' but the word 'refrigerator' would be a more accurate word for the room I spent more time in. It was January and so very cold that I wore two pairs of socks, I also kept my anorak and woolly hat on all the time I was there, plus I took a rolled up sleeping bag in and rested my feet on it and off of their bitterly cold floor and a blanket to cover my legs. Depite it being so bitterly cold, I continued. I was that dedicated and determined. The building there was an old Victorian Army building and heat was not available. Some months later it was all back to the central library and heat! I researched the pages of the Evening News from 1944 to the end of 1959.

During my library days, the Portsmouth Guildhall which had become a Trust found my web page and asked me in for a chat. They were keen to use a few spare rooms at the guildhall and make an exhibition of local popular music. I decided to introduce them to Dave Allen. He worked tirelessly and filled all the walls and corridor with the photos and history of Portsmouth's popular music history. Over the recent years it has blossomed into a fantastic sight. More recently in charge there are Nigel Grundy and Phil Freeman.

In 2011 Dave decided to gather all we had researched and include the 1950's and 1960's section in a book. 1000 were printed at his expense and were all sold with a small profit going to local music charities. He very kindly added my name to the book but I was not really involved in the production. It was called Dave & Mick's Pompey Pop Pix. Nine years later I took the lead and organised the publication of a follow up covering from 1970 to 1999. This time called Dave & Mick's MORE Pompey Pop Pix.

Song-writing, Writing and Acting

I have dabbled with song-writing for many years, and I was good friends with Tony Hutchins and his sister Gill early in the 1960's. He was guitarist in a group called the Crestas and I sometimes went to their practice nights. In those days I had little or no knowledge of writing music. I offered them lyrics without music but nothing developed from that.

Then with the For-Tunes I wrote a few that they recorded as demos. One called Tell little Linda was a reply song to the track recorded be Frank Kelly and the Hunters called 'I Saw Linda Yesterday.' It was played live a few times. Then Ron Hughes suggested I wrote a song called 'Cheap and Nasty Woman' which I did. I think we recorded that too, but now all trace of the recording and the lyric have disappeared, thankfully.

I gathered together some recording equipment to do my own demos at home. I bought a Tascam 8 track reel-to-reel record deck, and a Studiomaster mixing desk from the Strings guitar Centre, which Shakin' Jimmy kindly carried to my van. It was that heavy! After a year or so that equipment was replaced with a Roland digital recorder.Modern music-makers may consider me a bit of a dinosaur as I still use a very old method to write songs.

I was able to compose a music track with a keyboard workstation, save it as a MIDI file and load that into a very old version of Cubase on an almost prehistoric Atari 1040 computer to add layers of other instruments and make an arrangement. It's a process I have used many times and therefore I am very familiar with it. I have looked many times at more up to date ways to make a track on and a computer, without playing an instrument, but it would be like learning a new language, so I have purposely avoided it. Once this was done I record it onto my 8 track digital recorder. I was usually able to sing the melody and make a reasonable demo.

I was lucky sometime to get friends with good singing voices to record demos of them for me in my home studio. Dave Jackman Browne and John Paul McCrohon were happy and kind enough to give up their time and talent. My main lyric collaborator was someone I met through an organisation called BASCA (British Songwriters and Composers Association!)

Some very good songs were written with lyrics from Rosalind Winton, songs I am very pleased with and proud of. We even tried a number of times to write musicals but sadly we were unable to complete them. Rosalind and I entered a song called 'A Beautiful Lady' which was about the Titanic, into the Portsmouth Music Festival Competition, which John Paul kindly came along to the Portsmouth Grammar School to sing live to the judges. He did an excellent job too but we were not 'placed.'

Despite all my efforts I have never had any success in getting any of my songs recorded and released on a commercial record. I have sent demos off to various recording artists but the majority of them just ignore me.

There is however, one classic gem in my memory. I went to the Portsmouth Guildhall to see a particular singer that I liked and decided to drop off in the booking office a CD with a number of my songs on it. I went and saw and enjoyed the show and then in the following days forgot all about the CD. It just slipped out of my mind. About a month later my phone rang and asked for me by name, to which I owned up. He said something like 'Hello, this is Daniel O'Donnell, I'd just like that thank you for sending me your CD. I have played the songs and think they are very good but I don't think any are my style so can't use them, thanks anyway!'

I was gobsmacked. I think I grunted a couple of times as he spoke. OK thanks and put the receiver down. How stupid was that. I should have kept him talking and sussed out just what he really wanted and made him remember me in some way. Was that the hand of fame, fortune and fate sticking two fingers up at me? Maybe we'll never know. Yet another 'almost' moment.

In an effort to improve my song writing skills I have attended three residential song writing courses. First was during the 1980's on a farm in Essex, and to inspire us the leader was Kink Ray Davies, now a knight! It was a four and a half - five day course. One of the others on the course was a former recording singer Lene Lovich whose song Lucky Numbers made the charts, and also Hammer Horrors film actress Barbara Shelley.

Then some five or so years later another similar course in the middle of Dartmoor at a place called Totleigh Barton, a really very nice location. Again Ray Davies was leading us and he said he remembered me from the previous time. Here we had to take turns in cooking meals, and washing up after the meal. The last one I went on was back at Totleigh and this time our leader was Barry Mason. He was the lyricist of "Delilah", "The Last Waltz" and loads more with musician Les Reed.

I wrote a number of songs at all three, the early ones were

forgettable but of those written at Totleigh, there were a few that I still like. As of today I have written almost 250 songs, many of them I am very happy with. Some were lyrics from collaborators and many were words of my own with all music composed by me. Alas fame and fortune, and some celebrity to record one, has eluded me.

Another thing I got into early in the 1980's was writing. I signed on at the South Downs College for a 10 week course and then another. Next at Cowplain School another continuous weekly meeting run by Keir Cheatam. He was very encouraging and didn't charge anything. Sadly he died just a few years later. More recently, I have been a member of writers@lovedean. Enjoyable times with a local group of very enthusiastic writers.

I liked to write stories and not anything like a lengthy novel, mainly because a short story is quick and reasonably easy to write, and an occasional poem along with song lyrics. So in 2014 I self-published a book with a selection of my writings. It was called, "My Six Minute Stories, so far." I had just 75 printed and gave them away free to friends.

I had made contact with a lyric writer named Colin Grant through a Buddy Holly and the Crickets appreciation Society. After a few tries at collaboration, we played with the idea of writing a musical but neither of us had a clue how to do it. So I decided the best way to find out was to join one of the local groups. The South Downe Musical Society rehearsed at Portchester Village Hall and that was near so it was them I tried.

By the end of the 20th century, I had gained enough on stage hours and confidence, or so I thought. A far cry from those childhood days when I wouldn't say boo to anything! I thought I was ready for another adventure. This was the next challenge I unwittingly and very naively slipped into. I had wanted to write a musical so decided I needed to find out how they ran one and what they were all about from the inside. I joined the SDMS, but purely as a member of the chorus.

For my audition I had to sing backed by a pianist, and they seemed to like what they heard or were very hard up for older men. I think the latter may have been the case. I sang on stage at the Kings Theatre and the Ferneham Hall in Fareham on 5 or 6 productions between 2000 and 2005. I did have a few lines to say sometimes but was mainly happy to be back in the chorus. Showboat, Carmen, George M, Carousel, Sweet Charity were some of the shows I took part in. I helped backstage on a few shows moving props and scenery. Fiddler on the Roof was my last on stage show at the glorious Kings Theatre in 2005.

It was a very exacting process and there were some very talented actors and singers in the company who could have lived in the professional theatre world. It was something that I was glad to have done, but in hind sight, I sometimes wonder what possessed me to do it. Their productions were approached in a very professional way. Sometimes, fraught rehearsals and the pressure of two evening rehearsals a week in the month before shows was a struggle. A full week at the theatre in show week was the routine with dress rehearsal and then seven or eight shows.

The productions cost many thousands of pounds to put on. This included the hire of scenery, costumes, musicians, a performance license, and the theatre and programme charges. Well known shows were always played and most of the company were nice people and easy to get on with. However there was just one nameless thorn on the stage full of roses. I realise now that I wasn't really up to the high standard of many of the on-stage cast, all of whom were unpaid with day jobs. There were also many back-stage volunteers to support. It seemed like being back at work again with a very demanding schedule, but it was five years of my life I shall treasure and never forget. Also during my SDMS days my 60th birthday arrived and I invited 80 plus guests to a gathering at the Marriot Hotel. They included all of my God Children's family and about 40 from the SDMS plus a number of other friends from over the years. We had music, food and dancing and the whole night was a great success and very memorable.

Strangely, it was while I was with SDMS I met Brian Hodgkins and he also had an interest in writing and performing musicals. What's more, he had a script and a full set of lyrics, but no music. He was not a musician. When he told me of this and said he was looking for someone to add music, I jumped at the chance.

It was about a Portsmouth legend called John Pounds, who many will know ran a type of school for the poor kids from his cobblers shop in old Portsmouth centuries ago. It was me who named it 'Pounds of love' with the very best of intentions but a search on You Tube brings up all sorts of unsavoury items!

After a few months I had written all the songs and recorded demos of each one in my home studio. John Paul and Sheila Birt helped out with some vocals and I did most of them and the final result was encouraging.

Brian had got to know people at St George's Church again in Old Portsmouth, who were keen on singing and acting. We persuaded them to learn a few of the songs and also had made contact with officials at John Pounds Church. They allowed us, with our new singing friends, to video/film four of the songs in their mock up of John Pounds shop in the garden alongside the church. It was a wonderful sunny day and all went very well and the result can be seen on You Tube. We hiked the show around many of the local music and am dram groups but no one was interested. So, to this day the whole show has never been premièred.

My own musical tastes over the years have been quite wide. There is very little music I don't like. I have always listened to the song before deciding if I liked the singer. The song seemed to have been more important to me.

There have been exceptions. From the start Buddy Holly and the Crickets were always high on my list together with many of the 1950's Rock'n'rollers. I had a liking for harmony singing too, also a number of doo wop groups and Danny & the Juniors and The Fleetwoods were not everybody's favourites but were mine also Peter Paul and Mary. Through the 60's and 70's many songs and styles took over. I suppose more than ten minutes of steel drums and bagpipes is enough for most people but my tastes have grown and have always been very wide. For me trying to write a musical was an enjoyable challenge that sadly failed to interest any one.

But to quote the lines of a Joe Walsh song, Life's Been Good To Me.

Looking back I know that both of my main schools have been demolished. One has houses on it and on the other they built a brand-new hospital. The Honky Tonk is now an apartment block. The Spring Inn is also houses. Many of the clubs and pubs we played are now long gone. Despite all that, these days I make every effort to get out and see live music at the few remaining venues around the area.

Having grown up through the 1950's 60's and 70's that is the music I have played loved and is ingrained in me. Sadly from 1980 or so the music grew away from me and I have little time for modern music with a few special exceptions. I have met some very clever musicians and as often as I can go to see and their live music. Three particular bands/groups, call them what you will, namely The Men from Montgomery, Scarlet Town and Tuxedo Junction are favourites of mine. All are experienced and clever musicians that I have known for years. I must also add the Dave Pearson Big Band Orchestra who play excellent music on Sunday lunchtimes at the Hilsea Lido Blue Lagoon. The Barley Mow Pub in Southsea is another favourite venue. One can sit and listen in comfort.

One exception during the 1990's was when I got into the music of a very talented American singer/pianist named Gerard Kenny. He wrote some great songs, among them "New York New York, so good they named it twice", and the theme to Minder "I Could Be So Good For You," and many more and sung songs of Cole Porter, Lerner & Loewe and many other musical classics. He was living in East Sussex and I went to many of his shows and got to know him well. Even well enough to be invited to birthday parties and other gatherings. All that has now come to an end as he recently retired due ill health but is still in Sussex.

Over the years there have been romances, far too many to mention. Hold on, I said I was being honest? OK a few romances, but I didn't marry or have children and that would have been a life changer too! My branch of the family tree will end with me when I do. I would probably have spent my working day at a job I put up with just to bring home money to feed a family and not have been involved in the local music world. Fortunately I have been reasonably healthy and enjoyed much of my time.

I do believe I have had a lucky life, so far! I have met and worked with some very likeable and talented people over the years. From my early days, we in the For-Tunes still have regular gathering once or twice a year at the Good Companion on the Eastern Road, and we are still all good companions. Nigel Baker from my Jamie's Kin days also joins us there. Some time back Ron Hughes came up with the suggestion we call our gatherings 'PDR's' which with a smile he explained meant 'Pre Death Re-union.' The Soul Society did have one reunion a few years back. And of course these days many of us are still in contact through the internet.

I'm lucky to have lived in my present house for the majority of my life. I always say it's in an ideal position. I have the hill behind me, and beyond that the countryside. In front I have a supermarket and shops, then the motorway. I can go east to Brighton or west to Southampton or South to the grand City of Portsmouth. To my left I have that brand-new hospital, and a few miles to my right there's a crematorium! What more could I want or need?

Many of the people I have met in my early years have become life-long good friends and I am so grateful for that.

Regrets? Now there's a loaded question! It's what our American friends would call a 'curved ball' Coming at you out of the blue unexpectedly and hitting you hard and strong in the penalty area to use a soccer term, although I would prefer to use the word football.

I expect many people have regrets for things they wanted to do but never got around to it. Plans they made that were never fulfilled. When you're young some people have all manner of plans and ideas as to what they want to do but me? I seemed to glide through those early years quite easily and mindlessly. It wasn't until I got to about 40 when I started making money with photography. Capricorns are supposed to be late starters, all depending on which book you believe! I wish I had been a better musician, and kept up those piano lessons as a youngster. I can read music but sight reading has never been my strong point but I managed to busk my way through most of the time. Having one of my songs recorded by a 'name' would have been a bonus.

I have been called by a few different names through my life, most of them OK ! But one that seems to fit, I hope after reading this tome you will agree, and that word is 'historian.'

During 2019 I was contacted by people from the Isle of Wight who wanted to create a piece of artwork in mosaic form.I had to send them an outline drawing of my hand. Anyone who was on stage for the three 1960's IOW Festivals was contacted. The final design would probably amount to dozens of hands. I sent off my drawing and in 2020 the artwork was completed and I was interviewed for a film about it. So, another small mark to leave behind, another stroke of luck. So as for 'almost' at least I tried, I made an effort, and enjoyed it all.

Where are they now?

Happily, most of the fellow musicians and friends I have known are still living in and around the Portsmouth Area. Some are a little further away. Shellee Lee is now in Florida, Ray King in Germany. Dave Gautrey followed Rikki Farr to the USA and now lives in California and Geoff Davis in Spain. Ray Holloway and Ricky Martin both spent a few years in the Far East but have now returned to the old country.

I am happy to say I am still in touch with most of them. Sadly though some have gone and their book, or should I say Manuscript of life has reached its finale curtain way before their time.

To name a few, Don David, Paul Spooner, Brian Kemp, Andy Scarisbrick, Roy Huggett, Don Golding, Fred Illingworth and Nobby Glover. So I dedicate my musical memories to them. I am still here and able to write these words. I am the lucky one.

Photos

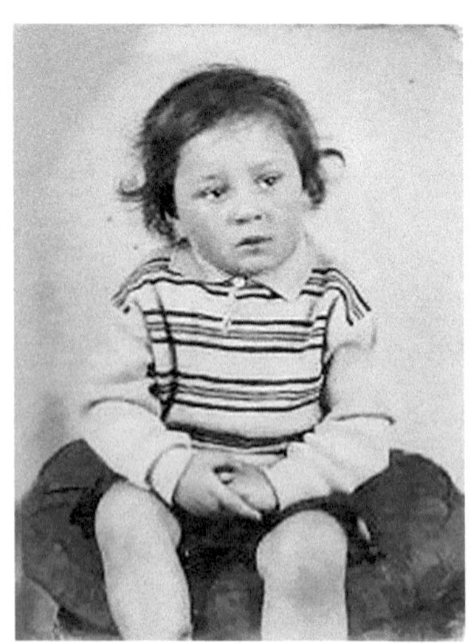

Early days – A long time ago

Early days – A long time ago

Rehearsal night

Packing up after the first gig

School gig photo

Evening News photo taken in my house

Josie in her splendour

Paul with Ken, Ron and Dave in Ricky's

Paul Spooner

Josie on stage

The Hamble Album label

Ready for the off at my house

At a recording session

The Portchester Castle photos

Still Rampant after all these years – the band that just keeps giving…

I love, and I think readers do too, 'then and now' pictures. Usually they are of places. But I particularly enjoy them when they are of people.

I especially relish them when they come from readers with a delicious sense of humour. Take a bow Portsmouth musician and one of the leading authorities on the history of popular music in the city, Mick Cooper. Have a look at the picture on the right and then on the left. The five likely lads, right, were a pop/beat combo called The Rampant around in Portsmouth in the 1960's. The publicity picture was taken half a century ago at Portchester Castle.

Fifty years on and they are all still alive and this week got together to recreate the original picture. Mick, who played Hammond organ and is on the far right in both, says: 'Unfortunately there is scaffolding all over the keep entrance, but I think English Heritage put it up to hold the five of us up and in position without our Zimmers. 'All five of us have regular get-togethers that we call PDRs. This stands for Pre Death Reunion. Each time we meet we each put sixpence in a tin. The one still around when the rest are gone gets the tin.'

Peter Richardson aka Ritchie Peters, Ron Hughes, Ken Hughes, Don Golding, Mick Cooper.

Bob Hind Portsmouth NEWS August 2017

Social Committee Presents a
Coming Up Dance
with
DEEP PURPLE
Juicy Lucy
Heaven
830-1·00
12/6 (10/- NUS)

Soul Society on the Tricorn

Heaven

Heaven

Strange meeting

Driving home through France from a holiday in Spain, Mr. Albert Elsegood, of Wallington Road, Copnor, was somewhat startled as he rounded a bend near Chartres.

For passing him on the other side of the road was a Portsmouth Corporation double-decker bus.

Said Mr. Elsegood: "It was quite a shock to see a Portsmouth bus hammering along in France. It was certainly causing some excitement among the locals, who had never seen a double-decker before."

When Mr. Elsegood (49) and his wife returned to Portsmouth, they read in THE NEWS the story about the party of young people from Liphook who were driving the ex-Corporation vehicle to Spain for a holiday.

After the show...

Scattered over the fields after the Island Pop Festival are mounds of empty cans.

2nd iow festival of music friday
the nice
bonzo dog band
eclection
edgar broughton
free
blonde on blonde
gypsy
heaven

2nd iow festival of music sat
the who
moody blues
fat mattress
family
marsha hunt
and white trash
pretty things
blodwyn pig
aynsley dunbar
king crimson
joe cocker

2nd iow festival of music sunday
bob dylan
the band
richie havens
julie felix
third ear band
pentangle
tom paxton
gary farr
indo jazz fusions
liverpool scene

The trio at the Spring Inn Sholing

Thyen Clacton with Shelly

The entertainers at Clacton

The beginning at the Honky Tonk

The beginning at the Honky Tonk

Our Nero's debut with Roy Castle, and Merrick keeping watch

Me with Dave, Chris and Jim

Geoff working to a packed house

Geoff, me, Nobby and Fred

Me with Fred, Nobby and Geoff

Honky Tonk days

Honky Tonk days

Honky Tonk days

A clever photo taken by our good friend Mike Scadden at the Honky Tonk

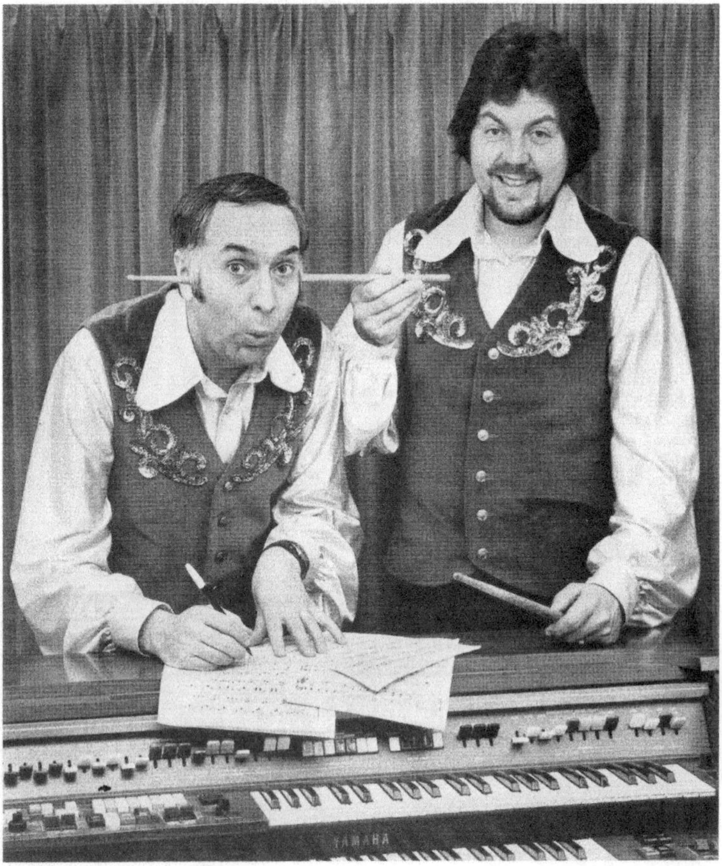

MICK and "CLUMP"

The GEE DEES

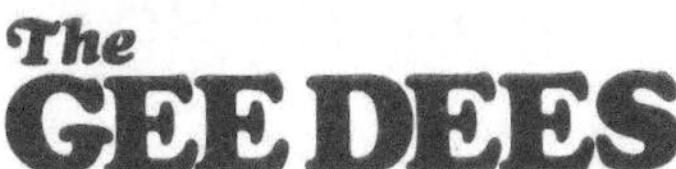

ORGAN & DRUMS PLUS VOCALS DUO
MUSIC FOR ANY OCCASION, ANYWHERE

TELEPHONE MICK NOW ON
COSHAM (0705) 371018

Duo and Solo days

Duo and Solo days

Duo and Solo days

My football books

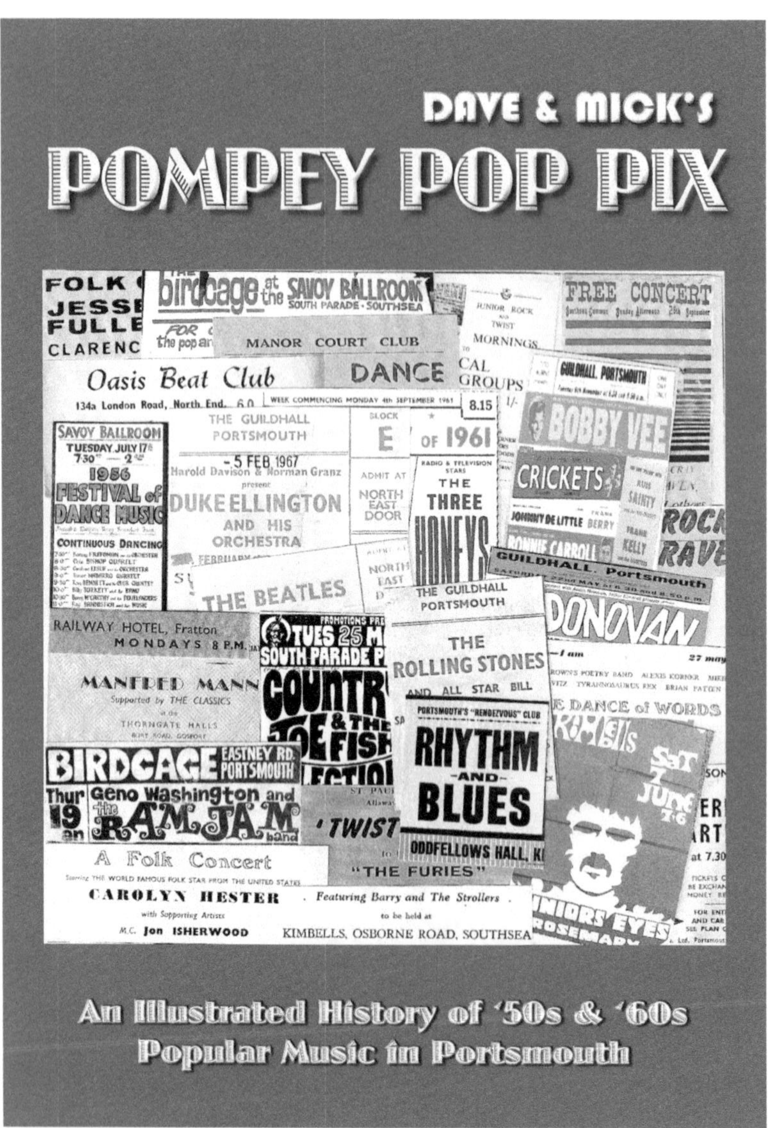

20th Century books

20th Century books

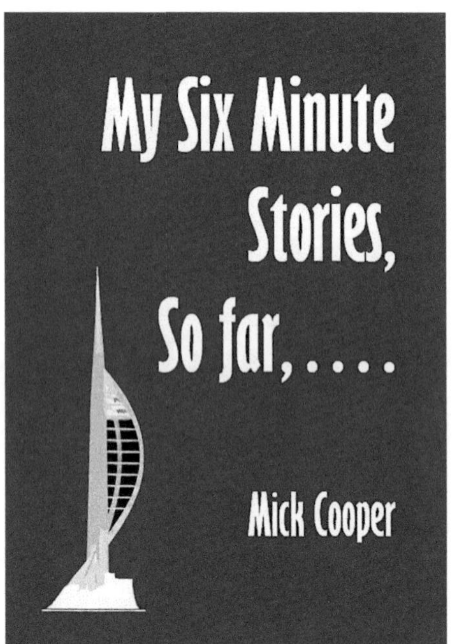

20th Century books

With Sonny Curtis in the Nashville motel

With Paul Cronin and his wife at the DIY store near Melbourne

Standing of the stage of the Grand 'Ole Opry Nashville

At the original Ryman Auditorium Nashville

With the Crickets, Gordon Payne, Joe B Mauldin and Jerry Allison

Me, the Actor, or more correctly 'the walk on'

That's me on the right and the horse on the left,
so easy to confuse the two.

Happy hippie days

A dress up day

My favourite NEWS photo

With a real beard in Fiddler on the roof

THE GRAMOPHONE CO. LTD. · ALL RIGHTS OF THE MANUFACTURER AND OF THE OWNER OF THE RECORDED WORK RESERVED · UNAUTHORISED PUBLIC PERFORMANCE BROADCASTING AND COPYING OF THIS RECORD PROHIBITED
COLUMBIA
45 R.P.M.
PEDRO MUSIC
7XCA 32041
DB 8394
SOLD IN U.K. SUBJECT TO RESALE PRICE CONDITIONS SEE PRICE LISTS
℗ 1968
EVERYBODY WANTS TO GO TO HEAVEN
(Coben—Kluger)
THE KARLINS
Arranged Geoff Love
with Geoff Love and
His Orchestra
MADE IN GT. BRITAIN

MARCA REGISTRADA · MFG'D BY DECCA RECORDS, INC., NEW YORK, U.S.A.
DECCA
RECORD NO.
9-30434
45-100442
2:26
Singing
with Instrumental
Accompaniment
THAT'LL BE THE DAY
(Jerry Allison-Buddy Holly-Norman Petty)
BUDDY HOLLY
And
THE THREE TUNES

MARCA REGISTRADA · MFG'D BY DECCA RECORDS, INC., NEW YORK, U.S.A.
DECCA
RECORD NO.
9-30650
(100,443)
(2:16)
From Decca Album
"THAT'LL BE
THE DAY"
HI - FI
DL 8707
Singing With
Instrumental
Accompaniment
GIRL ON MY MIND
(Jim Denny)
BUDDY HOLLY
And
THE THREE TUNES

the Original FOR-TUNES,
with"Ritchie Peters".
Say Now, (Kendrick).

the Original FOR-TUNES,
with"Ritchie Peters".
Tell Little Linda,
(Kendrick).

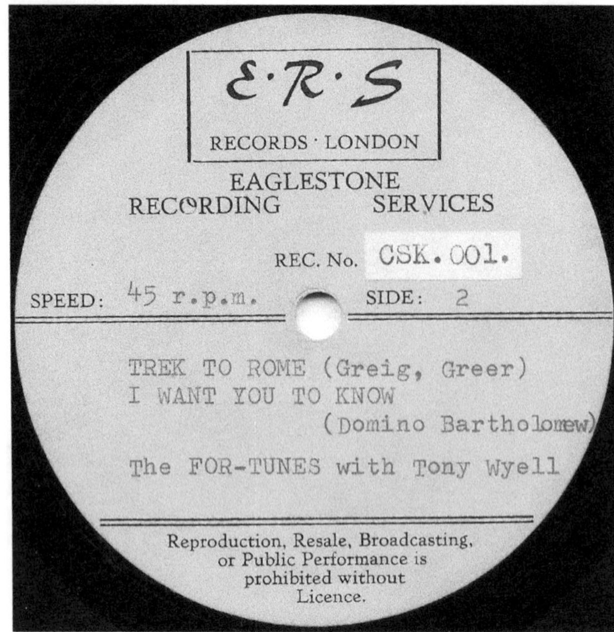
E·R·S
RECORDS · LONDON
EAGLESTONE
RECORDING SERVICES
REC. No. CSK.001.
SPEED: 45 r.p.m.
SIDE: 2
TREK TO ROME (Greig, Greer)
I WANT YOU TO KNOW
(Domino Bartholomew)
The FOR-TUNES with Tony Wyell
Reproduction, Resale, Broadcasting,
or Public Performance is
prohibited without
Licence.

E·R·S
RECORDS · LONDON
EAGLESTONE
RECORDING SERVICES
REC. No. CSK.001.
SPEED: 45 r.p.m.
SIDE: 1
LERGI Pt. 3 (Hughes, Hughes, Cawte)
GRANDFATHER'S CLOCK (Work)
The FOR-TUNES with Tony Wyell.
Reproduction, Resale, Broadcasting,
or Public Performance is
prohibited without
Licence.

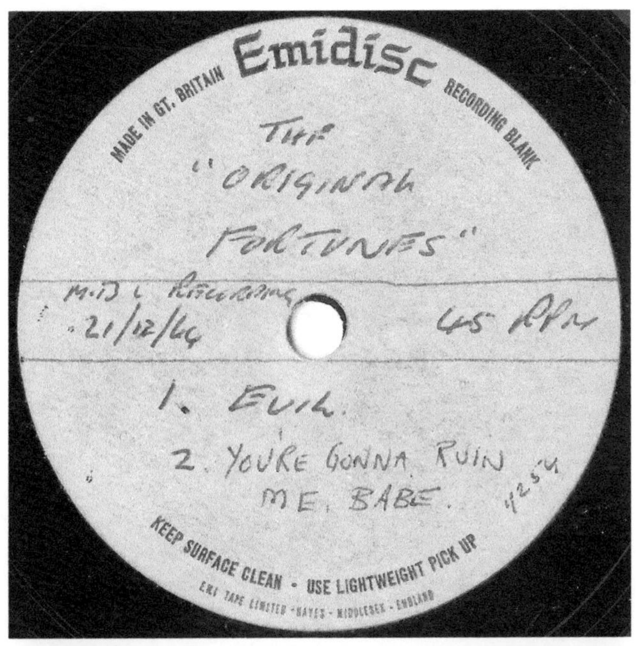
Emidisc
MADE IN GT. BRITAIN
RECORDING BLANK
THE "ORIGINAL FORTUNES"
21/12/64
45 RPM
1. EVIL.
2. YOU'RE GONNA RUIN ME. BABE.
KEEP SURFACE CLEAN - USE LIGHTWEIGHT PICK UP
E.M.I. TAPE LIMITED - HAYES - MIDDLESEX - ENGLAND

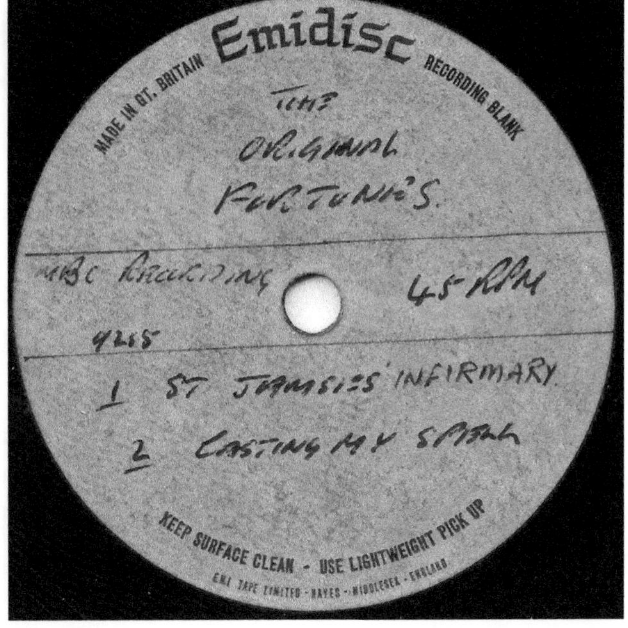
Emidisc
MADE IN GT. BRITAIN
RECORDING BLANK
THE ORIGINAL FORTUNES.
45 RPM
1 ST JAMES'S INFIRMARY.
2 CASTING MY SPELL
KEEP SURFACE CLEAN - USE LIGHTWEIGHT PICK UP
E.M.I. TAPE LIMITED - HAYES - MIDDLESEX - ENGLAND

45
THE FORTUNES

Emidisc
MADE IN GT. BRITAIN
RECORDING BLANK
DISC CUT BY
EDEN STUDIOS LTD
01-546 5577
45 r.p.m.
"WHITE DOVE"
(Andy Scarisbrick)
HEAVEN
KEEP SURFACE CLEAN - USE LIGHTWEIGHT PICK UP
E.M.I. TAPE LIMITED - HAYES - MIDDLESEX - ENGLAND

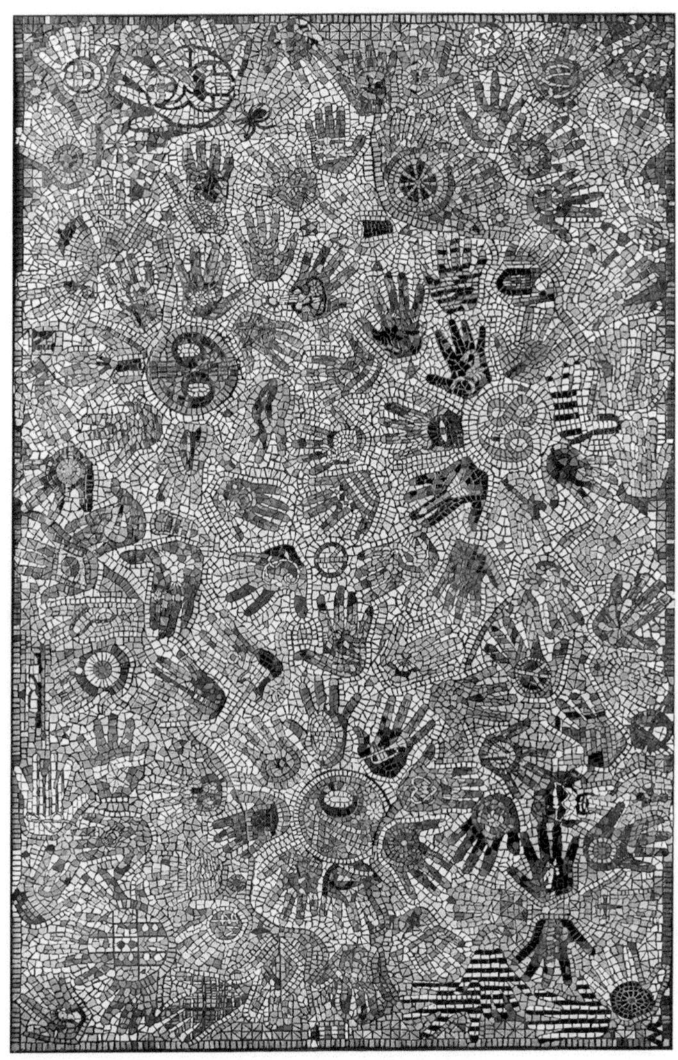

During 2019 I was contacted by people from the Isle of Wight who wanted to create a piece of artwork in mosaic form. I had to send them an outline drawing of my hand. Anyone who was on stage for the three 1960's IOW Festivals was contacted.

I sent off my drawing and in 2020 the artwork was completed.